Monitoring for Outcomes in Community Driven Projects

THIS WORK IS PUBLISHED BY
ACADEMIC FOUNDATION, NEW DELHI
IN ARRANGEMENT WITH
THE INTERNATIONAL BANK FOR RECONSTRUCTION
AND DEVELOPMENT / THE WORLD BANK GROUP

The authors:

ASHIS MONDAL is a well-known development professional in the field of community based natural resources management and community managed livelihoods initiatives. He is the founder Director of a reputed NGO, Action for Social Advancement (ASA), based in Bhopal, Madhya Pradesh, India. He is associated with several international organisations as expert in community demand driven initiatives and has authored more than 20 technical papers.

SOMA DUTTA is a development consultant, advising, researching and consulting on issues related to rural development, livelihoods, and rural and renewable energy. She has been associated with a number of developmental initiatives, both at national and international levels, providing support in project formulation, appraisal and implementation. For the last decade or so, she has also been providing support to a number of NGOs in research and documentation, strategic planning, fund raising and review of programmes.

Monitoring for Outcomes in Community Driven Projects

Using a Learning Based Approach

ASHIS MONDAL • SOMA DUTTA

THE WORLD BANK

ACADEMIC FOUNDATION

Published in 2007
by
ACADEMIC FOUNDATION
4772-73 / 23 Bharat Ram Road, (23 Ansari Road),
Darya Ganj, New Delhi - 110 002 (India).
Telephone: 23245001 / 02 / 03 / 04.
Fax: +91-11-23245005.
E-mail: academic@vsnl.com
Internet: www.academicfoundation.com

Monitoring for Outcomes in Community Driven Projects: Using a Learning Based Approach
by Ashis Mondal and Soma Dutta

ISBN-13: 978-81-7188-585-5
ISBN-10: 81-7188-585-3

Printed and bound in India.

Contents

List of Tables, Figures, Boxes and Annexures

TABLES

FIGURES

BOXES

ANNEXURES

Acknowledgements

There are many individuals and institutions that have played critical roles and without whom the work would not have been possible. We wish to express our sincere gratitude to all who supported us in this endeavour.

We are particularly grateful to the Social Development Unit, SASES, The World Bank, New Delhi for encouraging ASA to take up the assignment, which has provided us new insights into the complex linkages between people and their roles in enriching project outcomes. Our special thanks to Shankar Narayanan, coordinator of this assignment from the World Bank, for his continuous encouragement, unflagging enthusiasm and valuable inputs into the process. But for him, it would have been impossible to interest the large number of stakeholders who were involved in the process of developing the guidebook.

We are grateful to the project teams of the following World Bank projects who shared information, ideas and documents with us:

District Poverty Initiative Project, Andhra Pradesh.

District Poverty Initiative Project, Madhya Pradesh.

Karnataka Community-Based Tank Management Project.

Karnataka Rural Water Supply and Sanitation Project (*Jal Nirmal*).

Karnataka Watershed Development Project (*Sujala*).

Kerala Rural Water Supply and Sanitation Project (*Jalanidhi*).

Madhya Pradesh Forestry Project.

Rural Women's Empowerment Project (*Swashakti*), Madhya Pradesh.

Comments on drafts and additional material were gratefully received from the following World Bank staff and consultants: Ghanasham V. Abhyankar; Junaid Kamal Ahmad; Mary Bitekerezo; Samik Sundar Das; Karine Fourmond; Mirella Hernani; R.R. Mohan; Nilanjana Mukherjee; Daniel Murphy; Daniel Owen; Uma Rani; Salimah Samji; Daniel M. Sellen; Mridula Singh; Varalakshmi Vemuru; Warren Waters; and Mark C. Woodward.

Finally, we would like to thank all those who have worked in this project as consultants and have contributed to the opening up of new realms of analysis and insights to the topic in discussion. We are grateful to Dr. Astad Pastakia and Amod Khanna (Core Group Members) for their inputs and constructive criticism into the numerous drafts of the document, and Kalyan Paul of Grassroots, Ravinder Bhalla of FERAL and Sangeeta Agarwal for their inputs.

Action for Social Advancement (ASA),
Bhopal

Acronyms

ABF	Activity Based Federation
ABG	Activity Based Group
AIJ	Association of Independent Journalists
AP-DPIP	Andhra Pradesh District Poverty Initiatives Project
APD	Assistant Project Director
APM	Assistant Project Manager
ARR	Action Required Report
ASA	Action for Social Advancement
BGs	Beneficiary Groups
CBO	Community Based Organisations
CC	Community Coordinator
CDD	Community-Driven Development
CIGs	Common Interest Groups
CIP	Community Infrastructure Project
CLG	Community Learning Group
CMIS	Computerised Management Information System
CPML	Concurrent Process Monitoring and Learning
DLG	District Learning Group
DLL	Double-Loop Learning
DM&LC	District Monitoring and Learning Coordinator
DPIP	District Poverty Initiatives Project
DPM	District Project Manager
DPMU	District Project Management Unit
DPU	District Project Unit
EA	Environmental Assessment
FGDs	Focus Group Discussions
GIS	Geographical Information System
GoI	Government of India
GoTN	Government of Tamil Nadu
GP	*Gram Panchayat*
IDI	Institutional Development Indicators
IEC	Information, Education and Communication
ILG	Institutional Learning Group
IPQA	Implementation Phase Quadrilateral Agreement
ISDS	Integrated Safeguards Data Sheet
ISRO	Indian Space Research Organisation
KDP	Kecamatan Development Project
KRWSS	Kerala Rural Water Supply and Sanitation Programme
LFA	Logical Framework Analysis
LGE&RD	Local Government, Elections and Rural Development Department
LGs	Learning Groups
LME	Learning-based M&E System
M,E&L	Monitoring, Evaluation and Learning
M&E	Monitoring and Evaluation
MCSC	Mandal (sub-district) Community Support Cell
MIS	Management Information System
MS	*Mandal Samakhya*
NGO	Non-governmental Organisation
NMC	National Management Consultants
NWFP	North Western Frontier Province
PAD	Project Appraisal Document
PD	Project Director
PDOs	Project Development Objectives
PFTs	Project Facilitating Teams

PID	Project Information Document
PITA	Planning, Implementation Tripartite Agreement
PM	Process Monitoring
PML	Participatory Monitoring and Learning
PMT	Process Monitoring Team
PMU	Project Management Unit
PRA	Participatory Rural Appraisal
SERP	Society for Elimination of Rural Poverty
SHGs	Self-Help Groups
SLL	Single-Loop Learning
SO	Support Organisation
SOCHURSOD	Society for Human Rights and Social Development
SOPE	Status of Projects in Execution
SPMU	State Project Management Unit
SPU	State Project Unit
SSIs	Semi Structured Interviews
SWAP	Sujala Watershed Project
TLL	Triple-Loop Learning
TNEPRP	Tamil Nadu Empowerment and Poverty Reduction Project
ToR	Terms of Reference
VDC	Village Development Committee
VO	Village Organisation
VPRC	Village Poverty Reduction Committee
VWSC	Village Water and Sanitation Committee
WSP	Water & Sanitation Program

Preface

Within the World Bank, community driven development (CDD) is among the fastest growing mechanisms for channelling development assistance. CDD refers to an approach where communities have direct control over key project decisions as well as management for investment funds. A unique element of the design of these projects is that the communities, project functionaries and other stakeholders have an opportunity to learn from the project experience as they go along, and use the learning to improve the project outcomes.

In the context of CDD projects, monitoring and evaluation can be much more than a reporting mechanism, and can contribute significantly towards advancing the CDD goals. This guidebook is all *about improving the impact of CDD projects using* Monitoring and Evaluation (M&E) *as a management tool*. It advocates a 'learning-based' M&E system, which involves various stakeholders in the monitoring process on an ongoing basis in a manner that ensures learning for all. The guidebook explains what a learning-based M&E (LME) system is, demonstrates how such systems work and how the use of LME can help improve project performance, through case studies and examples, and suggests practical strategies on operationalising these within the existing CDD project framework.

This guidebook is designed specifically to assist the World Bank CDD project task teams and the project implementing agencies with their M&E responsibilities. Nonetheless, the concepts and approaches can be applied in development sector projects in general.

This guidebook has been developed by Action for Social Advancement (ASA), an Indian NGO, over the period of last two years or so. It has its genesis in an action research project on Participatory Monitoring & Learning supported by the South Asia Sector for Environment and Social Development (SASES) in 2002. The action research project was undertaken with six community-based rural development projects in India and implemented by two agencies, ASA, Bhopal and

India Network for Participatory Irrigation Management (IndiaNPIM), New Delhi. The ASA experiment was carried out in three World Bank assisted projects in Madhya Pradesh. The IndiaNPIM experiment was carried out by two field based NGOs, Foundation for Ecological Research Action and Learning (FERAL), Pondicherry and Grassroots, Ranikhet.

- The guidebook has been developed through an iterative process of consultation with its potential users: task teams from the World Bank, project managers and field staff, consultants and experts on M&E, and NGOs.

- It builds upon the lessons from other initiatives that have experimented with participatory monitoring and learning approaches, drawing from existing documentation as well as consultations with CDD project staff and communities.

We do hope that the readers of this guidebook will find it useful in improving the effectiveness of M&E systems of CDD projects within the World Bank as well as outside. This document should however be looked at as a starting point, rather than a prescription for how to integrate learning into the M&E systems of CDD projects.

Section I

Introducing the Learning-based M&E System

CHAPTER 1

Introducing the Guidebook

1.1 About the Guidebook

Community driven development (CDD), in the World Bank parlance, refers to an approach where communities have direct control over key project decisions as well as management of investment funds. The CDD approach treats poor people as assets and partners in the development process, building on their institutions and resources. Monitoring and evaluation (M&E) in the CDD context can potentially be much more than an input-output-outcome monitoring and a reporting mechanism. This guidebook is all about improving the implementation of CDD projects using M&E as a management tool. It is built on the contention that a 'learning-based' M&E system, which involves different project management levels and other stakeholders in a continuous process of 'learning', can help the project management make course corrections, guiding project strategy on an ongoing basis, ultimately leading to better project outcomes.

Box 1.1

This Guidebook

- **Is all about improving the implementation of CDD projects using M&E as a management tool.**
- **Advocates a learning-based M&E system that involves stakeholders at various levels in the monitoring process—in a manner that ensures learning for all on an ongoing basis.**
- **Is designed specifically in the context of CDD projects for World Bank: task teams at the World Bank, project managers, M&E staff and others who are involved in the implementation of CDD projects.**

A learning-based monitoring and evaluation system (LME) is an approach to M&E that:

- Facilitates a process of learning on a continuous basis.
- Provides timely inputs into management decisions at the local and central levels.
- Ensures a response mechanism that enables project strategies to be adjusted to emerging lessons and changing environments.
- Contributes towards making development process more demand responsive, inclusive, empowerment-oriented and sustainable by bringing in the interests and voices of broader stakeholder groups more systematically in discussing project strategies and performance.

The guidebook demonstrates:

- how a learning-based M&E (LME) system can improve project outputs and outcomes for CDD projects,

Typical questions a regular M&E system is good at answering relate to *accountability* to donors:

- **Has the project worked?**
- **How has money been spent?**
- **Should the project continue?**

On the other hand, a learning-based M&E system can help you answer questions like:

- **What are the project's strengths and weaknesses?**
- **What are the implementation problems?**
- **Why have things worked, or not?**
- **What are the good practice issues?**

- details on how such systems work, factors that render some M&E systems better than others, and the critical questions to ask of M&E operations, and
- practical strategies on how this can be operationalised within the existing CDD project framework.

1.1.1 Who Can Use the Guidebook?

The guidebook is designed specifically for the following audiences:

- World Bank CDD project task teams, which supervise, make critical decisions and provide implementation support to the projects.
- Project managers, who are directly responsible for the implementation and day-to-day management of projects.
- Project functionaries, particularly the M&E staff, who have the responsibility of setting up and implementing M&E systems.
- Consultants and external resource persons, who are hired either by the World Bank or the project management to provide external assistance on various aspects of M&E.

1.2 The Basis of the Guidebook

1.2.1 M&E in CDD Projects

CDD is a major component of the broad empowerment agenda pursued by the World Bank. Specifically, CDD seeks to put local governments and rural and urban communities in the driver's seat, and gives them a new set of powers, rights and obligations. It does so by empowering communities; empowering local governments; refashioning management and control processes to support arms-length relationships between multiple centres of power; building capacity and improving accountability (Binswanger and Nguyen, 2005). As a development approach, CDD has the potential to improve efficiency and effectiveness of project outcomes and hence enhance chances of sustainability. The CDD approach has gained momentum significantly in the last few years, with the World Bank's lending in CDD projects increasing from $ 325 million in 1996 to $ 2 billion in 2003 (Mansuri and Rao, 2003).

At the same time, the CDD approach is being questioned by some. As articulated by Mansuri and Rao, some of the questions that have been raised in the context of the CDD approach are:

- Does community participation improve the targeting of private benefits?

- Are public goods created by CDD projects better targeted to the poor?
- Are they of higher quality, or better managed than similar public goods provided by the government through the traditional approach?
- Does participation lead to the empowerment of marginalised groups? In particular, does it lessen exclusion, increase the capacity of the collective action, and reduce the possibility that project benefits are captured by locally powerful elites?
- Are the characteristics of 'external agents' (donors, governments, NGOs and project facilitators) relevant for the quality of participation induced and/or for project success/failure?
- Can CDD projects be sustainably scaled up?

Responses to these questions could vary depending on a range of factors including the finer elements of project design, the sector in which the project is being implemented, and most importantly, the contextual specifics of the location where a CDD project is being implemented. With decentralised decision making being the cornerstone of CDD projects, the implementation arrangements need to be flexible and nurture local level decision making. The 10/90 Rule (10 per cent design/90 per cent implementation) that recognises the importance of 'learning by doing' and using learning to modify project design and implementation specifics as projects move forward, applies strongly to CDD projects.

Unfortunately, most existing monitoring and evaluation systems within the CDD projects do not shed much light on these issues, and there is not enough empirical evidence to either support or disagree with the kind of criticisms highlighted by Mansuri and Rao. An important shortcoming in CDD projects seems to be the inability of their M&E systems to systematically validate the hypotheses they are based on.

Two reasons could be attributed to this.

Firstly, CDD project designs in recent years have undergone major changes favouring decentralisation, with the recent projects becoming multi-dimensional and multi-sectoral, involving a wide range of stakeholders. With increasing focus on 'processes', the relationships within the more recent projects have become far more dynamic than earlier projects. Unfortunately, the project M&E systems within the World Bank and in general continue to remain focused largely on inputs monitoring, reporting more on 'compliance', that too most often limited to progress on achievement of inputs such as disbursements, number of sub-projects approved or implemented, etc. This approach does not provide the project managers and other stakeholders with an understanding of the success or failure of the project. Neither does it help to understand the *whys* of a particular phenomenon: why is a particular community poorly represented in the distribution of benefits; why do women's issues never feature in a *gram sabha* (village council) meeting; why do self-help groups promoted under a certain project lack momentum; why is the community passive towards a particular project component and so on.

Secondly, even in cases where efforts have been made to customise the M&E system to the needs of CDD projects, they have been hindered by a lack of motivation/skills or both on the part of the borrower to implement it in true spirit—possibly because they lack the conviction that such customised M&E systems can indeed help these projects achieve their objectives better.

M&E systems that were truly responsive to the information needs of the decision makers were found to be more the exception than the rule in the portfolio of CDD projects reviewed for preparing this guidebook. Even where adequate attention was paid to M&E in project design, the implementation phase focused on only a few elements of this design, e.g. progress monitoring which is essentially tracking the project activities or inputs. Rarely did the team come across an M&E system that enabled all levels of the organisation to effectively carry out their assigned functions.

Why is this So?

Firstly, there seems to be a tendency among many project decision makers to use observations/interactions during field visits and telephone discussions to take decisions where required rather than invest in setting up a system that would last much longer than a commonly used *ad hoc* approach to decision making would.

Secondly, rarely does a task team consider the setting up of an M&E system to be a high priority activity. M&E is meant to satisfy project clearance requirements of having an LFA (Logical Framework Analysis), indicators for success and failure, etc. that would be measured at baseline, mid-term and end-of-project to arrive at conclusions about how successful the project was in achieving its stated objectives. In most cases, it is a necessary project requirement that has to be accommodated and therefore is the focus of attention only when all other important activities and consultancy contracts have been dealt with.

Thirdly, task teams and the borrower teams do not realise how important a carefully designed M&E is for effective project management. Very rarely is M&E considered an important way of helping project functionaries learn about progress or lack thereof and use this knowledge to take appropriate corrective action during the course of the project. Project Director of one of the projects reviewed actually quipped, "Why are you talking about monitoring even before activities have been implemented?"

The lack of attention to quality aspects in M&E in CDD projects reviewed is one of the malaises that this guidebook aims to analyse and address. The team interviewed a number of project managers to understand the bottlenecks that they face in involving stakeholders in the M&E process. Some of the commonly faced bottlenecks include an across-the-board lack of conviction about the value-addition such as an approach to M&E; the tendency to use community consultations as a guise for participatory monitoring; implementing M&E as a top-down system more for reporting than for the benefit of project communities; lack of project agency ownership and understanding of the M&E design and implementation; and a fear of accountability and defensiveness towards monitoring in general.

Notwithstanding the problems with the M&E systems in the majority of CDD projects, there are exceptions where the M&E systems have been designed and implemented in a manner that they have contributed effectively to the needs of the project, helping the various project stakeholders to learn from the project experience, enabling course corrections in strategy and finally, contributing to better achievement of project outcomes. Some of the notable experiences include the M&E System of Kecamatan Development Project (KDP) in Indonesia (Wong, 2003), Process Monitoring in the NWFP Community Infrastructure Project in Pakistan (Viloria and Hosain), the Kerala Rural Water Supply and Sanitation Project and the Andhra Pradesh District Poverty Initiatives Project (AP-DPIP) in India. The guidebook discusses these and other case studies on effective M&E strategies, identifying factors that either facilitate or inhibit the setting up of effective learning-based M&E systems in projects.

1.2.2 The Significance of a Learning-based M&E System in CDD Projects

CDD projects, by their very design, are all about communities taking charge of their own development. In order to be useful, their M&E systems need to be harmonised with this underlying philosophy: they need to be responsive to the needs of the project communities; serve as a management tool for the project functionaries; and finally, contribute towards advancing the CDD goals.

The traditional implementation focused M&E systems within the World Bank are geared towards 'compliance' monitoring, assessing how well a project is being executed. M&E focuses on inputs and outputs (physical and financial) as they relate to predefined project targets, staffing levels and expenditure. While these M&E systems provide useful information to decision-makers in terms of *measuring* levels and changes in impacts, they are less effective in understanding *processes*—that is, how a particular intervention instigates a series of events that ultimately result in the observed impact. They also miss out on a critical and unique element that CDD projects encompass: the ongoing process of learning. In addition to reporting on quantitative aspects, a good M&E design should ensure that the *learning* from implementation experience, interaction with participating communities amongst other stakeholders and the measures put in place for transparency, independent agency monitoring, etc. help project management to use this learning for ensuring better achievement of project outcomes. Hence, a well functioning M&E system should integrate data-oriented, quantitative techniques complementarily with 'soft', less formal learning-based monitoring approaches.

1.3 Using the Guidebook

This guidebook is designed specifically to assist CDD project task teams and project implementing agencies with responsibilities they are likely to have for monitoring and evaluation. It is developed in a manner that is anchored into the World Bank programming arrangements at different stages of the project cycle.[1] Experiences from ongoing and completed projects have been utilised as case

1. The World Bank project cycle is described in Annexure A-1.

studies, as relevant. Where needed, references to other information sources are included.

Finally, it must be mentioned that a guidebook is not a panacea for the problems faced in M&E systems, and for that matter, for any system. It is a set of suggestions, drawn from specific experiences and good practices that worked well in certain situations. As people managing projects, you will need to examine these suggestions in the specific context of your own experiences, projects and concerns, adapt them as required. This work is only a beginning in this direction, and as a body of experience builds up, this document will need to be refined and perhaps overhauled completely, to retain its usefulness.

Figure 1.1

Structure of the Guidebook

Introduction to the guidebook and basics of the LME approach	M&E in CDD projects, the significance of learning in CDD projects, introducing the LME approach: definition, best practices.
↓	
Strategies for integrating learning in M&E systems of CDD projects	Practical suggestions on how to adopt the approach in CDD projects.
↓	
Achieving better project outcomes through learning based M&E	Case studies where the LME approach has been used for better achievement of project outcomes.

Further reading:

Binswanger, Hans P. and Tuu-Van Nguyen (2005). "A Step By Step Guide to Scale Up Community Development", Presented at the Development International workshop on *African Water Laws: Plural Legislative Frameworks for Rural Water Management in Africa*, 26-28 January, Johannesburg: South Africa.

Binswanger, Hans P. and Swaminathan S. Aiyar (2003). *Scaling Up Community Driven Development: Theoretical Underpinnings and Program Design Implications,* Draft dated August 2003.

Mansuri, Ghazala and Vijayendra Rao (2003). *Evaluating Community Based and Community Driven Development: A Critical Review of Evidence*, Development Research Group, The World Bank, September.

Narayan, D. (1993). "Participatory Evaluation: Tools for Managing Change in Water and Sanitation", *World Bank Technical Paper* No. 207, Washington DC: The World Bank.

Viloria, J. (SASIN) and M. Hosain (WSP-SA). *Transforming Organisations by Learning and Adaptation: Process Monitoring in the NWFP Community Infrastructure Project (CIP)*, Participatory Monitoring & Evaluation, Good Practice & Lessons Learned.

Wong, Susan (2003). *Indonesia Kecamatan Development Program: Building a Monitoring and Evaluation System for a Large-scale Community-driven Development Program,* Environment and Social Development Unit, East Asia and Pacific Region, World Bank, May.

CHAPTER 2

A Learning-based Approach to Monitoring and Evaluation

Box 2.1

Key Messages in this Chapter

- A learning-based M&E system engages stakeholders in monitoring, encouraging a process of learning for all on a continuous basis.
- The cornerstone of this approach is its emphasis on organisational learning, which requires institutionalisation of learning forums at all levels.
- A learning-based M&E system must move beyond answering 'what is happening', and address questions on 'why', 'so what', and 'what to do next'.
- As a project manager, you need to take concrete measures to nurture commitment to learning within your project and organisation.

2.1 What is a Learning-based M&E System?

A learning-based M&E system (LME) can be defined as a process of collaborative problem-solving through the generation and use of knowledge that leads to corrective action by involving all levels of users in shared decision making. It is a process through which stakeholders at various levels engage in learning from implementing a particular project, programme or policy. In practical terms, it is a set of participatory tools and methods for

- measuring,
- assessing,
- reporting on, documenting and ultimately
- improving organisation's performance through *shared, institutional learning*.

Box 2.2

What Comprises the LME?

- It is a collaborative process where stakeholders monitor their own performance so as to be able to learn to improve their own performance.
- It is a process where communities and implementing agencies decide on how progress should be measured and what corrective measures need to be taken to improve implementation.
- It is a system that facilitates learning and information flow—bottom up and top down.
- It focuses on processes and outcomes, rather than inputs and outputs.
- It requires the management to provide space for and be open to constructive criticism from project stakeholders.

A key point of departure from traditional M&E is that in LME, it is the stakeholders who are directly or indirectly involved in a programme—take part in selecting the indicators to measure changes, in collecting information and in evaluating findings.

In terms of definition, the boundaries of LME are fairly broad and the term can be used to encompass a wide range of tools, methodologies and approaches. Common elements that are understood to describe LME include 'monitoring own performance', 'process orientation', 'openness towards constructive criticism', and 'communities deciding on how to define and monitor progress', etc. (Box 2.2).

Box 2.3

An Example of Traditional M&E *versus* a Learning-based M&E System

Organisation A

In a livelihoods project, the field staff collects information on the number of sub-projects approved in each project village on a monthly basis, and reports these figures to their district project manager. The district project manager adds up the numbers, and sends a monthly report to the state office which sends them to the donor. Very few people actually look at the data to see what it is saying: Are incomes per family increasing or decreasing? Will the project reach its objective to reduce poverty? What is the sustainability of sub-projects? How can project staff and community members work together to make the project a success?

Organisation B

Every month, field staff collects information on the number of sub-projects approved in each project village. Periodically, they also rate the performance of these groups. Community representatives and project field staff discuss this information during their monthly review meetings. These data are then sent to project headquarters for forwarding to the donor. When the growth in the number of sub-projects approved declined, the local stakeholders tried to figure out *why* by asking clients. With a simple change in strategy, they were able to once again increase the number of sub-projects approved. Monitoring information was used within the organisation to improve the programme, and also to report to the donor.

Source: Adapted from CORE 2004.

2.2 The 'Learning Dimension' of a Learning-based M&E System

The emphasis on *organisational learning* is what distinguishes a learning-based M&E system from other M&E approaches. The learning process supports existing skills and resources, i.e. it builds on what people already know and do, using and developing people's current abilities and skills to monitor their own progress. The learning process must encompass the project communities, the field level functionaries, as well as the project management. LME can be seen as a cyclical process of overlapping circles where participants define success; collect information; refine and verify the results; reflect and build on what is working; identify lessons learned and obstacles and take corrective action. An essential feature of this learning cycle is for stakeholder groups to reflect continuously on the impact of their action and where the process is leading them, learning from their own successes and failures. And it is this learning process that creates conducive conditions for change and action.

The learning cycle has been conceptualised by many (Argyris and Schön, 1978; Ward, 1997). Commonly used frameworks are 'levels of learning' and 'learning loops'. Argyris and Schön, (1978) use the term 'single-loop learning' (SLL) to describe the kind of learning routine monitoring leads to, which is functional, low order and maintenance-oriented.

> "There is a single feedback loop which connects detected outcomes of action to organisational strategies and assumptions which are modified so as to keep the organisational performance within the range set by organisational norms. The norms themselves... remain unchanged."

A higher level or the 'double–loop learning' (DLL) is said to be taking place when organisations find, that in order to maintain performance, or even to survive, the norms themselves need to be questioned. This kind of questioning leads to learning called double–loop learning (DLL):

> "...which occurs when error is detected and corrected in ways that involve the modification of an organisation's underlying norms, policies, and objectives."

Figure 2.1

Types of Organisational Learning

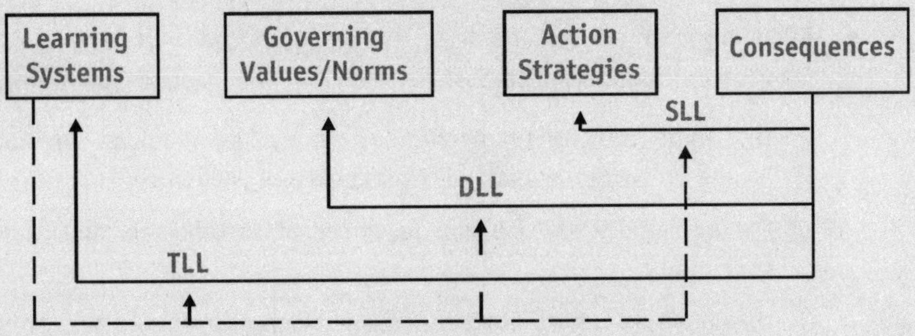

Source: Based on Argyris (1993) and Issacs (1993) in Chhokar (1999).

Building on this, others have conceptualised a third type of learning called triple-loop learning (TLL). They maintain that while double-loop learning answers the question, "what are the alternative ways of seeing the situation that could free me to act more effectively?", triple-loop learning would answer the question "what is leading me and others to have a predisposition to learn in this way at all?" It takes the enquiry much deeper into the nature of learning itself (Issacs, 1993, in Chhokar, 1999). Top management that seeks to answer this question becomes more aware of formal and informal systems of learning within its organisation and may also end up re-designing its learning systems.

2.3 Implementing a Learning-based M&E System: Some Common Pitfalls

- Defining participation. Defining who the stakeholders are, who should be involved in LME and to what extent they can and want to be involved can be tricky. Experience shows that a monitoring system

Box 2.4

Levels of Organisational Learning

When organisations use M&E information for:

- **routine monitoring: it represents single-loop learning,**
- **project planning: it represents single or double-loop learning,**
- **re-designing policies and re-looking objectives: it represents double-loop learning, and**
- **raising questions regarding organisational learning systems: it represents triple-loop learning.**

based on active participation of the grassroots is only feasible if the project really corresponds to people's needs.

- Encompassing conflicting stakes. Stakeholders look at (and hence measure) project results, outcomes and impacts differently. How these differing (and often competing) stakeholder claims and perspectives are negotiated and resolved, especially when particular groups and/or individuals are less powerful *vis-à-vis* others, remains a critical question.
- Assuming that all stakeholders will be interested in taking part in monitoring. Successful establishment of LME will depend on:
  a) the willingness and commitment of all stakeholders, including having a conducive external (institutional) environment;
  b) the availability of time and resources of stakeholders and project staff; and
  c) the extent of trust that the stakeholders, especially the project communities have in the agency initiating LME.
- Imposing inappropriate indicators and methods in an effort to standardise and save time.
- Being unclear about how information will be used, and by whom; collecting unnecessary information.

2.4 The Learning-based M&E System in Action

The learning-based M&E system, or selected elements of it, has been used successfully in a number of World Bank supported projects. After reviewing a number of projects, six have been analysed and presented as detailed case studies in Section III of this guidebook. These projects are:

- Kecamatan Development Project (KDP), Indonesia;
- Community Infrastructure Project (CIP), Pakistan;
- Kerala Rural Water Supply and Sanitation Programme (KRWSS), India;

- Sujala Watershed Project, Karnataka, India;
- District Poverty Initiatives Project (DPIP), Andhra Pradesh, India; and
- District Poverty Initiatives Project (DPIP), Madhya Pradesh, India.

2.4.1 Best Practices in Application of LME

The case studies discussed in Section III demonstrate a range of good practices in making a learning-based monitoring and evaluation system work in projects. Part of the reason why these strategies worked well can be traced back to the specific situations they were applied in: a socio-cultural context receptive towards community-based monitoring; a project with decentralised, community-led operations; an external monitoring agency with a track-record for objectivity; senior project management convinced of the usefulness of a good M&E system and so on. There are however certain common elements that run through all of these, which emerge as good practices for learning-based M&E systems. Here we try to summarise these:

- Ensure that there are clearly defined points for review, consolidation, and action based on reporting of M&E findings (sections 4.1, 4.3, 4.4, 4.6).

A direct and 'visible' link between M&E findings and actions taken is a must to create a buy-in for and sustainability of a learning-based M&E system. Decentralisation of monitoring functions is useful to ensure that M&E findings get translated into decisions with minimum loss of time, with specific accountabilities attached to them.

- Encourage critical reflection through learning forums at all project levels (sections 4.1, 4.2, 4.3).

Creation of learning forum at all levels is a must. To the extent possible, use existing opportunities within the project structures to encourage learning. The findings emerging at each level must be analysed and shared with the concerned group/individuals who are responsible to act on it.

- Use external monitoring agency for process monitoring (sections 4.1, 4.4, 4.5, 4.6).

For process monitoring, 'external' agencies are more appropriate. They can maintain objectivity in their findings and analysis. They are seen as 'neutral' by and enjoy the confidence of all project staff and other stakeholders. They also enjoy a level of freedom that the project staff does not. This was amply borne out by all the case studies. The implementing agency however has to play a critical role in terms of creating an across-the-board awareness about the importance of monitoring (conveying that monitoring is for learning and not fault finding), internalise its feedback into regular monitoring systems, ensure that actions are taken on the findings, and in general, encourage a learning culture within the organisation.

- Broad-base project information among stakeholders (sections 4.1, 4.3, 4.5, 4.6).

In large projects, broad-basing project information is an effective monitoring tool. Providing necessary information in the public domain is very critical for the stakeholders to keep track of the project.

- Build capacities of the monitoring agencies (sections 4.2, 4.3, 4.6).

It is useful to continuously upgrade the skills of the monitoring agency staff, both internal as well as external. Capacity building areas include developing an understanding about the project and its procedures, participatory research, data management, etc.

2.5 Making Learning-based M&E Systems Work: What Can You Do to Encourage Learning within Your Projects and Organisations?

As a project manager, you need to take concrete measures to build commitment to learning.

- Make learning a central and visible part of the organisation's mission and strategies.
- Speak about the importance of learning publicly and frequently.
- Build capacities and commitment at different levels to accept LME feedback constructively and take positive action for improvement.
- Be sensitive to the needs, workloads, sentiments, etc. of the project staff and help them to build confidence in the system.
- Encourage experimentation and adaptation within the LME system.
- Make optimum use of existing learning opportunities within the system.
- Ensure that appraisal systems reflect learning actions and outcomes.
- Create activities and events which provide opportunities for learning for people in the organisation.
- As a leader, bring in issues, ideas and concerns from outside the organisation and encourage staff to examine them.

Box 2.5

How Learning-oriented is your M&E System?

In addition to reporting on what is happening within the project, does the existing M&E system help you answer:

- **Why is it happening? Is this an operational issue or a strategic one?**
- **What are the implications for the project? Is the project likely to achieve its objectives? Are there any trade-offs between disbursements, quantitative target achievements and qualitative outcomes?**
- **What should we do next?**

If not, a learning-based approach to M&E could be one of the strategies that you need to consider.

The following sections show you how.

Further reading on participatory monitoring and evaluation:

Action for Social Advancement (ASA) (2004). Project completion Report of *Equitable and Sustainable Natural Resources Management through Participatory Monitoring,* A World Bank Supported Initiative in Madhya Pradesh, Bhopal.

Argyris, C. and D.A. Schön (1978). *Organisational Learning: A Theory of Action Perspective,* Maryland: Addison-Wesley Reading.

Campos, Jennie and Francoise Coupal (1997). *Who are the Question-Makers? A Participatory Evaluation Handbook,* UNDP, Strategic Planning and Evaluation Unit, One United Nations, Plaza, New York.

Chhokar, J.S. (1999). "Building Learning Organisations" in Sasi Misra and P.G. Vijaya Sherry Chand (eds.), *Institution Building: An International Perspective on Management Education,* Delhi: Macmillan India Ltd.

Estrella, M. *et al.,* (eds.), (2000). *Learning from Change: Issues and Experience in Participatory Monitoring and Evaluation,* London: IT Publications IIED, *http://www.ids.ac.uk/ids/bookshop/wp/wp70.pdf.*

Estrella, M. and J. Gaventa (1998). "Who Counts Reality? Participatory Monitoring and Evaluation: A Literature Review", *IDS Working Paper* No. 70, Brighton: IDS.

Guijt, I and J. Gaventa (1998). *Participatory Monitoring and Evaluation: Learning from Change,* IDS Policy Briefing.

IIED (1998). *Participatory Monitoring and Evaluation,* PLA Notes No. 31, Sustainable Agriculture and Rural Livelihoods Programme, London: International Institute for Environment and Development.

IIRR (1998). *Participatory Monitoring and Evaluation: Experiences and Lessons,* Workshop Proceedings. Philippines: International Institute of Rural Reconstruction.

Narayan, D. (1993). "Participatory Evaluation: Tools for Managing Change in Water and Sanitation", *World Bank Technical Paper* No. 207, Washington DC: The World Bank.

Ward, Pene (1997). "Getting the Right End of the Stick: Participatory Monitoring and Evaluation in an Organizational Context", Paper for the International Workshop on *Participatory Monitoring and Evaluation: Experiences and Lessons,* Nov. 24-29, Philippines.

Websites:

World Bank: *www.worldbank.org/participation*

FAO: *http://www.fao.org/participation/default.htm*

GTZ: *http://www.gtz.de/participation/english/index.html*

DFID: *http://www.livelihoods.org*

Institute for Development Studies (IDS) on Participation: *http://www.ids.ac.uk/ids/particip*

IDS on P. Monitoring and Evaluation: *http://www.ids.ac.uk/ids/particip/research/pme.html*

ELDIS: *www.eldis.org/participation*

Monitoring and Evaluation news: *www.mande.co.uk*

Box 2.6

Summary of Application of LME in the Six Case Studies

	Project					
Particulars	*KDP*	*CIP*	*KRWSS*	*Sujala*	*AP-DPIP*	*MP-DPIP*
Location	Indonesia	Pakistan	Kerala (India)	Karnataka (India)	Andhra Pradesh (India)	Madhya Pradesh (India)
Project Period	1998-2006	1996-2003	1999-2006	2001-2007	2000-2008	2001-2006
Scale	Very large: $700 million; 28,000 villages	90 communities; 6 lakh beneficiaries	80-100 *Gram Panchayats;* 1304 beneficiary groups (BGs)	7 districts; 1270 villages; 4 lakh households	28 districts; 29 lakh beneficiaries	14 districts; 2908 villages
Objectives	Poverty alleviation, decentralised development	Upgrading infrastructure	Decentralised rural water supply and sanitation	Micro-watershed development	Poverty alleviation, organising poor for self-help	Poverty alleviation, organising poor for self-help through CIGs[1]
Implementing Agency	Government ministry	Government department	Government department	Government department	Autonomous society promoted by AP state government	Autonomous society promoted by MP state government
People's Contribution	No preset target, but the higher the contribution, the more favourably the village proposal is reviewed	20 per cent	25 per cent	10 per cent	10 per cent	15 per cent
LME Initiators/ Facilitators	Internal (project staff) and external (NGOs, consultants, journalists)	External team, part of the internal M&E system	External agency	External agency (Antrix corp., ISRO[2])	External agency (SOCHORSOD)[3]	External agency (ASA)
LME System Components/Tools	- Self-evaluation by village councils - Special community teams carry out social audits - NGO facilitated community monitoring - Grievance handling mechanism - Field consultants' monitoring - Newspaper reports by journalists	Process monitoring: - Case studies - Field notes - Visual demonstration	Process monitoring - Self-evaluation by BGs - Social audit by *Gram Panchayats* and BGs - Diagnostic meetings with BGs	Process monitoring: - Monthly field visits and meetings with field staff - Monthly report to head-office, - Monthly feedback to watershed committees	Process monitoring: - One to one meetings with DPMs - District level PM rounds with de-briefing and 'agree to do' commitments - Feed upwards to SPMU in PDs conference and World Bank Mission - Monitoring action taken in every subsequent meeting - Action taken reports	- Process monitoring starting with learning processes - CIG *milans* as learning forums - CIG *milan* (VDC) as governance tool

(contd...)

(...contd...)

Particulars	Project					
	KDP	*CIP*	*KRWSS*	*Sujala*	*AP-DPIP*	*MP-DPIP*
Learning Dimension	- Village level community groups share learnings at council and village meetings - Feedback from external agencies and grievance handling mechanism used for making project level changes	- Process monitoring working group (with people from different levels)	- The community forums broad-base project information, demystify technology-related issues and enable the community to clarify issues - Lessons learned through process monitoring in the early phases have been incorporated in subsequent ones.	State (M&L cell) district and village (watershed committee) levels	District and state level meetings	Village (CIG *milan*), district and state (PML cell) levels
Type of Learning[4]	Mostly single-loop learning	Mostly single-loop learning	Single and double-loop learning	Mostly single-loop learning	Mostly single-loop learning	Single, double and most importantly triple-loop learning
Impact	Very cost effective: 50 per cent cheaper than comparable public works; approach spreading to other sectors.	Focus shifted from targets and physical achievements to quality, transparency and accountability. Community mobilisation has become a key area of attention.	Helped to improve project design and policy, improved quality control, project ownership and accountability among the community groups, built capacities of the community groups for participatory governance.	Helped to guide project implementation, improved efficiency; useful diagnostic tool for trouble shooting. Helped to identify success stories.	Improved efficiency and effectiveness; built capacities of the community groups; improved transparency and accountability at all levels.	Improved governance at village level; improved capacity of community groups for local level planning; improved efficiency and impact on a pilot scale.

Notes:
1. Common Interest Groups (CIGs) are formed from among the poorest families within project villages, which put forward a sub-project proposal for funding from DPIP.
2. Indian Space Research Organisation.
3. Society for Human Rights and Social Development.
4. KDP, KRWSS and MP-DPIP had facilitated self-evaluation among the village communities and institutions. KDP, KRWSS and MP-DPIP laid stress on devolution of powers and had strong learning groups at the community/village level. As a result in these villages, the levels of empowerment and governance improved. KRWSS and MP-DPIP had examples of double-loop learning, which helped to bring about strategic/policy changes in those projects. In the rest of the projects where learning was mainly of the single-loop variety, the main benefits were on account of reduced costs, improved efficiency and effectiveness.

Section II

Strategies for Applying the Learning-based M&E Systems in CDD Projects

CHAPTER 3

Strategies for Operationalising a Learning-based M&E Systems in CDD Projects

3.1 Strategy 1: Think Through and Set up the Learning-based M&E System during the Project Design Stage

The project design stage is a crucial stage for a learning-based M&E system; this is when clarity on the purpose and scope of the system needs to be established. At this stage, there is a need to know

- who are the likely actors in the process,
- who the end users of the M&E will be,
- how the results will be used, and
- what is the process to be carried out.

Most project managers feel that it makes sense to introduce a learning-based M&E in early stages as it is easier to set it up during the design phase, when the rest of the project components, systems and procedures are being tied up, so that it can be integrated within the whole, and does not run as a separate system parallel to the regular data-based M&E. The framework for the learning-based M&E should be fleshed out during the appraisal stage, when the project is well defined,

Box 3.1

Strategies for Operationalising the LME System in CDD Projects

- Think through and set up the learning-based M&E system during the project design stage.
  - o Ensure that the design of the LME framework is in line with the local context.
  - o Engage a right person/agency to guide the borrower to develop the LME system design.
  - o Ensure clear documentation of the components of the system in the project documents.
  - o Field-test the proposed LME framework during pilot experiments.
- Use technical studies to guide project design.
- Provide necessary support to the borrower during the implementation phase.
  - o Demonstrate the value of LME to the borrower.
  - o Ensure that the necessary institutional setup and capacities are in place.
  - o Ensure that there is a direct link between M&E findings and actions taken.
- Provide capacity building and hand-holding support to the community during implementation stage.
- Identify, track and act upon unforeseen project issues.
- Use process monitoring as a management tool during project implementation.

Box 3.2

Setting Up the LME System during Project Design: Early Bird Advantages

- It helps all stakeholders identify their role right from the beginning, build consensus on what is being monitored, when, why and by whom.
- If it is not built in from the start, there may be little incentive to build it in later.
- It is important for the task teams and the borrowers to get into the learning mode as early as possible.
- Right at the outset, it is important to set out clearly what the project is going to measure its performance against. As the project evolves and is implemented, course corrections can be made.

Source: Survey with World Bank Task Team Leaders and CDD project managers.

Box 3.3

Organisational Readiness to Adopt the LME System: Questions You Need to Ask at Design Stage

- What potential pressures are encouraging the need for a learning-based M&E system and why?
- Who will own the system? Who will finally benefit from the system, and how much information do they really need?
- How will the system directly support the achievement of programme goals?
- How will the information generated under the LME system be integrated with regular, quantitative M&E system to present an integrated picture?
- How is the organisation likely to react to negative information generated by the system?
- Does the capacity exist to support the learning-based M&E system?

and the institutional arrangements are finalised.

Setting up the learning-based M&E system during the project design stage involves:

- Ensuring that the design of the LME framework is in line with the local context.
- Engaging a right person/agency to guide the borrower to develop the design.
- Ensuring clarity and proper documentation of the components of the LME system.
- Field-testing the proposed framework during the pilot experiments.

3.1.1 Ensuring that the Design of the LME Framework is in Line with the Local Context

How well a learning-based M&E system delivers the desired results and contributes to better achievement of project outcomes, is governed, to a very large extent, by factors external to the M&E system: the existing political and social context, the existing organisational capacity of the borrower etc., which must be reviewed before designing the LME system.

(a) How Does the Borrower's Past Experience and Organisational Culture Influence the Design of the Learning-based M&E System?

In order to ensure that the results expected of a learning-based M&E system are realistic and that the design is in line with the capabilities, the existing M&E system (people, systems, procedures, capacities) of the borrower and its various partners, should be reviewed. Aspects that influence this include:

- Organisational culture, attitude and experience with participatory approaches.
- The incentives of various stakeholders to monitor the performance of the project.
- Willingness on the part of the borrower to allocate resources for capacity building and implementing the system.

CDD projects work with a wide range of borrowers and the strategy appropriate for operationalising the LME system within a particular project/organisation can be quite different, depending on the organisational culture and responsiveness towards participation.

Type of Project Agency	*Focus of the LME Strategy*
Large, monolithic government departments that have no experience of working with communities, and have neither the inclination nor the skills to implement learning-based concepts and techniques.	• Demonstrating the concept of a learning-based M&E and its usefulness to the project staff, especially the top management in order to get a buy-in, for the concept. • Guidance in setting up the system. • Training and capacity building on the LME system. • Handholding support in implementing the system.
Organisations that have some interest in community interaction, but need considerable handholding support to operationalise learning-based M&E concepts and derive maximum utility from them	• Guidance in setting up the system· Training and capacity building on the LME system and participatory techniques. • Handholding support in implementing the system.
Organisations that have a culture of working with communities, are familiar with participatory approaches	Guidance in setting up and operationalising the system.

(b) How does the Political and Social Context of a Project Influence the LME System Design?

Understanding the context of the project is critical to setting up a learning-based M&E system. The key questions that determine the purpose and scope of a learning-based M&E system are:

- How hierarchical is the governance tradition in the project area?

The typical patron-beneficiary relationship common in traditional local governance may prevent involvement of certain sections of the society in the monitoring systems. On the other hand, a conducive socio-political situation can make positive difference in terms of openness towards new methods of learning. In the Kerala Rural Water Supply and Sanitation Project (KRWSS), the *gram panchayats* (village council) were already in a position to take up governance functions within the project because of the high level of political awareness in the state. Similarly, in the Indonesia Kecamatan Development Project (KDP), a poverty alleviation project, there was a strong political will for devolution of powers to the community level, and this greatly facilitated the acceptance of LME as a system of bottom-up learning. The autonomous status of the implementing agencies for DPIP also created a better atmosphere for the staff to accept PML and respond to the feedback in a proactive way (see chapter 4 for detailed case studies).

- Have any poverty alleviation projects been implemented in the region in the recent past? What was the level of participation of the community?

The Kerala Rural Water Supply and Sanitation Project (Jalanidhi) (for details, refer to chapter 4), has demonstrated a high degree of community's interest and ability to monitor the project. The project was built on the experience of an earlier, highly successful, state-implemented water and sanitation project, and hence the atmosphere and responsiveness of the community towards the project was very positive. Further, the *gram panchayats*, the primary monitoring agencies, are very active in local governance; used to handling large budgets.[1] For most, this project is another activity in the huge portfolio of activities that the *gram panchayat* is handling.

- What is the status of poor and vulnerable groups in the society?

Box 3.4

Creating Enabling Conditions for Women's Involvement

In order to include the voice of women in decision making processes within the project, the Maharashtra Rural Water and Sanitation project (Jalswarajya) project has instituted special mechanisms. Under the project, funds for planning and implementation of sub-projects are transferred directly to the *gram panchayat*. Before any money is released however, the *gram panchayat* is required to fulfil the following obligations:

- It has to form a Village Water and Sanitation Committee (VWSC) in which at least half the members are women.
- The *gram panchayat* is required to organise a *mahila gram sabha* (women's village council meeting) a day before the general *gram sabha*. The recommendations of the *mahila gram sabha* have to be placed before the *gram sabha* and if a sub-project proposal from the *mahila gram sabha* is rejected, the reasons for rejection have to be explicitly stated. Additionally, the *gram sabha* must have at least 50 per cent representation from women. Only if these conditions are fulfilled, the decision of the *gram sabha* on a sub-project is taken into consideration.
- A Women Empowerment Fund has been set up to build women's capacity to participate in the project, which links self-help groups (SHGs) for productive collaboration, provides skill building opportunities to SHGs and seed money to the poorest groups (identified by the *mahila gram sabha*).

"Giving these powers to women has brought in meaningful changes in the villages," says Hanumant Gunjal, a local leader. Ms. Kalavati, one of the SHG members, admitted that the women of the village never used to step out. Now they are actively involved in deciding on the water scheme that the village would forward to the Government. They have helped to dig soak pits for disposal of wastewater, build percolation tanks to replenish underground aquifers, and develop kitchen gardens that use household wastewater.

In societies where vulnerable groups including women are not economically and socially empowered, PML will need to incorporate special provisions to make sure that their voices are heard. At times project staff may need to act as their spokesperson and represent their views on the project processes.

3.1.2 Engaging a Right Person/agency to Guide the Borrower to Develop the LME Design

Designing a learning-based M&E system involves five critical elements, which need to be worked out during the project design stage:

- Establishing the purpose and scope of the system.
- Designing its components.
- Planning information gathering and analysis.
- Planning and establishing mechanisms for sharing of learning.
- Planning for necessary conditions and capacities.

Developing the design of the system is a complex task and needs considerable expertise. As a task team leader, you need to ensure that:

- Appropriate expertise is made available to guide the borrower to develop the LME system design. The expert may be an internal bank staff member or an external consultant.

1. In Kerala the majority of the government's annual plan outlay for rural development is directly spent through the *gram panchayat*. This is in contrast to many of the other states in India where the government departments are responsible for the implementation of rural development programmes and the funds are routed through these line departments.

- The expert has sufficient time, resources and flexibility to play his/her role effectively.
- The expert has the capability to receive and respond to inputs from both the World Bank design team as well as the borrower.
- The expert provides handholding support to the borrower to find right consulting agency to carry out various components of the learning-based M&E system: reviewing terms of reference (ToRs) of the consulting agency, facilitating the bidding process, periodically reviewing the outputs of the agency, etc. The capacity of the borrower to accomplish these tasks satisfactorily is often limited and many a time, the outputs delivered by the agencies are of little use to the project. Hence, assistance to the borrower for the above mentioned services can add considerable value in building borrowers' capacity.

3.1.3 Ensuring Clarity and Proper Documentation of the Components of the System

A basic requirement for the LME to be accepted and used is to ensure that it is not a stand-alone system, but operates within the overall M&E framework. In developing an integrated M&E system, it is important to use the two approaches as complementary. As a task team leader, at the design stage, you must

- Ensure clarity on each of the component of the system. The M&E framework, developed for

Box 3.5

An Integrated M&E Design: Sujala Watershed Project Karnataka

The Sujala Watershed Project, a community driven watershed development project, is being implemented in the state of Karnataka. The integrated monitoring, evaluation and learning (M,E&L) system is based on a combination of methods including satellite and ground based monitoring systems. It provides information on key issues, progress and performance, social and environmental impact, which are fed back into the decision making system. The M,E&L system is organised under two main categories:

- Concurrent monitoring comprising:
  - input/output monitoring (physical and financial progress monitoring through MIS): Largely quantitative in nature,
  - process monitoring which looks at key processes (awareness and sensitisation, participatory rural appraisal (PRA) and baseline, entry point activities, community-based organisations (CBO) formation, capacity building, SWAP (Sujala Watershed Action Plan) preparation, environmental and social screening, SWAP implementation, income generation activity and operations and maintenance (O&M) strategy), and
  - Self-assessment by the CBOs involved in the project.
- Impact assessment, which carries out in-depth assessment of critical project aspects, highlighted by the regular process monitoring (combination of quantitative and qualitative approaches). Periodic thematic studies are carried out, in addition to regular evaluations.

Reporting and learning systems include dissemination of findings through learning events, which are linked with the evolution of capacity building activities. Each district prepares a detailed six monthly progress report, which is consolidated into a single project progress report.

Figure 3.1

M,E&L System of Sujala Project

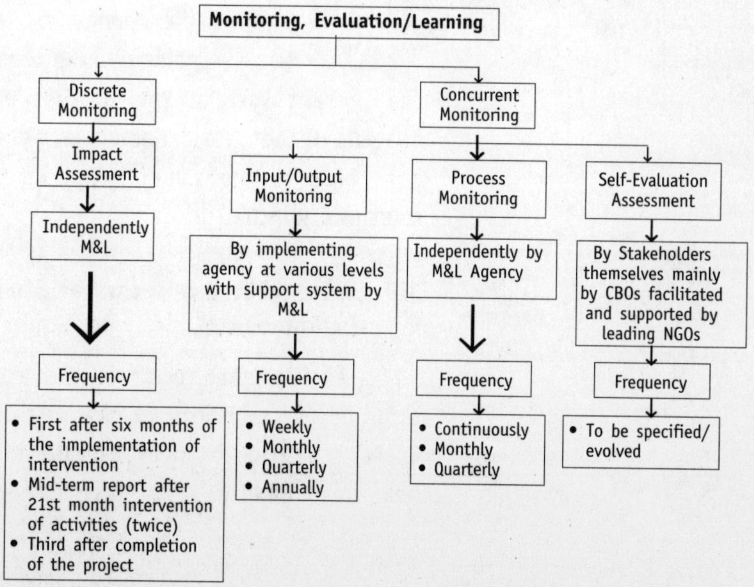

the project, must answer for each component: what to do, why to do, how to do, when and by whom and for whom.

- Ensure that the LME system is documented in adequate detail in the project documents.

The M&E framework of one of the recent CDD projects, the Tamil Nadu Empowerment and Poverty Reduction Project (TNEPRP), is presented in Annexure A-2 for reference.

After a project is approved, there are two main documents that are developed, and serve as a reference point for the subsequent operations, the Project Implementation Plan, or the PIP, prepared by the implementing agency, which serves as a guide throughout the implementation process, and the Project Appraisal Document, or the PAD, prepared by the World Bank, which is a public document and is used by the Bank staff for project management and monitoring. A suggested contents list for the M&E sections in the PAD and the PIP are included in Annexure A-3.

3.1.4 Field-test the Proposed Framework for the LME System during Pilot Experiments

The pilot experimentation phase, which precedes the main implementation phase of the project, is when the project components are field tested. Use this opportunity to test the M&E framework and incorporate learnings to modify the system, as required.

An example of the pilot phase contributing to shaping the M&E strategy in the main implementation stage of the project is the Kerala Jalanidhi Project (discussed in chapter 4). In the pilot phase of the project, the community's involvement in monitoring was limited to assisting the external process monitoring team in data collection and identification of problem areas. In the main project however, this was modified. A system has been put in place, wherein the community takes active part in the problem analysis and solution exploration process during process monitoring. In the present system, the process monitoring team carries out a comparative analysis of the data collected from various beneficiary groups (BGs), after which it goes back to the same groups to share and analyse the results and look for solutions jointly.

Box 3.6

Field Testing the LME Strategy during the Project Pilot Phase Helps in

- Creating an understanding and buy-in for the approach among the project stakeholders.
- Incorporating community perceptions in the M&E design: minimise surprises later!
- Helping all stakeholders to understand their roles and building their capacities.
- Fine-tuning the M&E strategy for the implementation phase.

3.2 Strategy 2: Use Technical Studies (Social, Institutional, Environmental, etc.) to Guide Project Design

An important function of a learning-based monitoring system at the design stage is to contribute to the setting up of the project development objectives, examine whether or not these are relevant, and whether the best action strategies have been identified for their achievement.

The primary function of M&E at this stage is to guide the project strategy. The PDOs are the cornerstone of the project design, with the entire project strategy evolving around them. Hence their importance and the need for them to be firmly rooted in ground reality cannot be overemphasised. Early interaction with the communities can play an important 'bridge role', connecting the macro and micro picture, and ensuring that there is no disconnect between the perceptions of the community, the project goals and the strategies planned to achieve them. As pointed out by a manager involved in a biodiversity project in Ghana, the project team worked intensively with the community during the project design stage to develop project impact indicators, which were included in the project document. Involving the community members early on in the process helped them understand the justification and strategy of the project better and are more active in implementing them (IFAD, 2002).

The pertinent question then is how to get a better sense of ground realities at the time of project design and what are the windows of opportunities available that can be used for this purpose. As part of the project design process, the borrower is required to get several studies conducted. The involvement of task team in these studies is intensive in terms of identification, designing the ToRs, selection of researchers, monitoring of studies and approving the final report. These studies are potentially the best options for understanding ground situation better, however, in reality, completion of these studies is often no more than a mere formality for both the bank and the borrower.

In order to ensure that the social studies reflect the ground reality and contribute towards guiding the project strategy, as a task team leader, you need to ensure that the studies answer the following questions:

- What is the root cause and level of poverty in the project region?
- What has been done so far to reduce it, with what results?
- What are the sectoral opportunities that the project can tap?
- Is the policy environment conducive for a CDD project?
- What are the community preparedness/conditions available for public-private partnership, role of civil society?
- What are the optimum and realistic expectations for this project?

Once you have made sure that the social studies address these issues, the logical step is to ensure that the findings of these studies are integrated into the project design.

When social assessment studies are conducted for your projects, keep in mind the following:

- What are the criteria for arriving at the specific themes for the social assessment studies?
- How do you ensure that the target community's interests are represented adequately in the social assessment studies?

- How will you ensure that the outputs from the social assessment studies are utilised for the project design?

3.3 Strategy 3: From Design to Operationalisation: Provide Necessary Support to the Borrower during Implementation Phase

An effective operationalisation and usage of a learning-based monitoring system requires conviction and buy-in among the project managers, and other necessary conditions and capacities within the project. A well-designed system can easily go astray in the absence of support during implementation. Depending on the capacity of the implementing agency, the Bank may need to provide continued support in this area.

- As a task team, what support are you providing to the borrower during implementation stage for the operationalisation of the LME system?
- You need to asses the capacity of the borrower in the beginning and make a clear plan of action on how you are going to support them, with what intensity, how long, and with what expected results.

3.3.1 Demonstrating to the Implementing Agency the Value of a Learning-based Approach to M&E

Having a high level 'champion' of the learning-based approach to M&E within the implementing agency can be a big advantage. When someone in authority has a stated commitment to organisational learning, it gets transmitted within the organisation. Understanding that making mistakes is an important part of the learning process, the champion can create room to manoeuvre while experiments take place.

- Getting a buy-in at the project management level can be achieved through sharing practical, positive examples from within and outside the country, cross project visits, workshops during design phase, etc.

Buy-in for the value of learning is further strengthened, when the project stakeholders at various levels are made aware that these findings are indeed being used by the project management.

- Ensure that there are communication mechanisms within the project to 'demonstrate' the effectiveness of the approach.

> **Box 3.7**
>
> **Specific Areas in Which Bank Support is Critical**
>
> - Demonstrating to the implementing agency the value of a learning-based approach to M&E.
> - Ensuring that the necessary institutional setup and capacities are in place.
> - Ensuring that there is a direct link between M&E findings and actions taken.

3.3.2 Ensuring that the Necessary Institutional Setup and Capacities are in Place

In order to ensure that a learning-based M&E is implemented effectively, necessary resources, capacities and structures must be in place. Meeting capacity building needs requires ensuring that M&E is carried out by the right people (either by hiring trained people/training own staff/hiring external consultants for specific inputs). It is also important to remove disincentives and introduce incentives for learning, ensuring that all stakeholders understand what is expected of them and assessing if they have necessary skills.

(a) Identify an appropriate agency to steer LME

A learning-based M&E system can either be externally led, internally led or adopt a joint approach.

Externally led M&E is organised and conducted by individuals/groups considered having no direct involvement or interest in the outcome of the project or initiative. They are commissioned by the project to give an objective and unbiased point of view and expected to achieve a balanced facilitation of opinions of all stakeholders.

It can be internally led, in which the activities are carried out mainly by those directly involved in project planning and implementation.

The third option, which is increasingly becoming popular, is a joint approach, which combines elements of internal and external M&E, and aims to assess the project from the viewpoint of both insiders and outsiders, with the underlying objective to achieve a more holistic perspective and involve a more diverse set of stakeholders (see section 4.1, 4.3, 4.4 for examples). In many cases, the external M&E agency serves as a facilitator-trainer for internal capacity building and sustainability of the M&E process.

Interaction with project agencies at different levels suggests that a learning-based M&E system is perhaps best led by an external agency, with support from project staff. While the process of acceptance of an external team may take painstakingly long, once this hurdle is crossed, project staff feels more comfortable dealing with an external agency that is considered neutral, with no stakes in the findings. Furthermore, it is simpler to shed organisational hierarchies and inculcate a learning mode in the minds of people, when meetings are facilitated by an external team. Having an external agency leading the effort also ensures objectivity, provides an outsider view, and enables in-depth analysis and assessment.

When an external agency is hired to steer a learning-based M&E system (IFAD, 2002), make sure that

- They are being used strategically, in ways that build local capacity and build on existing M&E.
- There is complete clarity on their tasks and responsibilities *vis-à-vis* the internal project staff (a sample ToR for an NGO monitoring project processes in the World Bank supported Kecamatan Development Program in Indonesia is included in Annexure A-3.4).
- Some continuity of the staff is maintained in order to minimise the need to reconcile to conflicting advice.

A high quality in M&E can be ensured only when firstly, staff selection is in line with the desired skills and attitudes, and secondly, the capacities and motivation of the M&E staff is built on a continuous basis. In Antrix, the external monitoring agency for Sujala watershed project, the M,E&L staff meets every month. In addition to reviewing progress, the staff meetings are also used to conduct training sessions on specific topics such as research methodologies, data analysis, facilitation skills, etc. In addition, Antrix organises six-monthly workshops for the M,E&L staff on special issues such as social inclusion that are of importance to the project. The staff also undergoes a rigorous training in data collection, analysis before any thematic study is launched, which ensures the quality of output.

Box 3.8

Skills Set Required to Handle Learning-based M&E Effectively

- Ideas for learning methods.
- Facilitation skills and knowledge of field tools.
- Data management including ability to assess implication of data for the project.
- Understanding of cross cutting issues of gender, poverty and environmental sustainability.
- Ability to develop a positive working relationship with all project units.

Box 3.9

Commonly Faced Disincentives for M&E Staff

- Lack of role clarity.
- Lack of clear understanding on how information will be used.
- Incentives linked only with physical/quantifiable indicators (no. of SHGs formed, disbursements made, no. of visits made, etc.).
- Frequent rotation of M&E staff
- Feeling of isolation in terms of recognition of their contribution towards achieving the project goal.

(b) Establish motivating conditions that encourage learning-based M&E

"Staff engaged in M&E is often used for a variety of *ad hoc* tasks, leaving them little time to focus on their real function. The poor stature of this staff compromises their ability to discuss issues in an open manner; where management does not want to hear about weaknesses in implementation, this information is often conveniently buried. There are few incentives to look beyond the superficial achievement of physical and financial targets."[2]

The above scenario describes a typical project situation. In most projects, unless the LME system is directly linked to performance, there is no real incentive to 'do process'. Especially at the field level, staff performance tends to be driven by the incentives that field staff has, and these are often not well aligned with the needs of the project. Vasan (2002) shows how facilitators, in the forest management projects she looked at, overlooked project goals when their personal incentives were in contradiction to them. Botchway (2001), studying participatory projects in North Ghana, notes that project facilitators are often quite vulnerable to manipulation and control by locally powerful individuals and groups because they are typically quite young, inadequately experienced, and poorly paid. For a project community, lack of follow up action on the part of the project agency after certain decisions have been taken at the village level, can be extremely de-motivating.

Putting in place incentives means offering stimuli that encourage M&E staff, project managers and project communities to view the learning-based M&E system as an opportunity to discuss problems openly, reflect critically, and make necessary changes in project strategy. Some of the incentives that can be used to encourage staff to take an active interest in monitoring include: clarity of

2. Extracted from Viloria and Hosain, *Transforming Organisations by Learning and Adaptation: Process Monitoring in the NWFP Community Infrastructure Project (CIP)*.

M&E responsibility in job descriptions and work-plans; salaries and other rewards; ensuring necessary support to carry out required learning-based monitoring activities and opportunities for professional development.

3.4 Strategy 4: Provide Capacity Building and Handholding Support to the Community during Implementation Stage

In order that the community is in a position to monitor quality, quantity and effectiveness of service delivery and hold the project implementation agencies accountable for their actions, it is important that the community receives support from the project in certain critical areas. In the CDD projects reviewed for preparation of this guidebook, the team came across several examples of the kind of support that enabled the community to perform the monitoring and 'watchdog functions'. Two such areas in which providing support to the community during the sub-project cycle are:

- broad-basing project information, and
- building the capacities of the CBOs to perform their project functions

Box 3.10

Incentives that Encourage Learning-based M&E Systems

- **Clarity of M&E responsibility in terms of clear job description, work plans.**
- **Financial and other rewards: appropriate salaries and other rewards such as vehicle use.**
- **Activity support: financial and other resources required to carry out M&E activities.**
- **Professional development for career achievement: training/ external learning opportunities.**
- **Recognition: acting on recommendations of staff, publicly recognising staff *via* competitions on best 'learning practices', encouraging staff to present learning experiences in public.**
- **Performance appraisal processes: equal focus on staff capacity to learn and innovate rather than only on achievement of quantitative targets.**
- **Demonstrating the use of M&E findings, making the data explicit and interesting by displaying in public boards and newsletters.**
- **Feedback: Informing data collectors and analysts how it has contributed to the project.**

3.4.1 Broad-basing Project Information

Communities need to be well informed about the project components, conditions, and terms of CDD projects. Wide public dissemination of this material helps to place control in the hands of communities, mitigate risks of manipulation by politicians, government officials, contracting agencies, and local elites. Access to complete project information also provides people a sound basis to voice their concerns and needs, which can be integrated into the project strategy.

CDD projects use a variety of tools for disseminating project information such as public meetings, wall paintings, hand-bills etc. In the Sujala Watershed Project, wall paintings in local language, using pictures and graphics, on walls of prominent buildings such as the *panchayat* hall/village school, etc. are used widely. The wall paintings also display details like unit rates for various activities, labour charges and project investment. This enables the project communities to have access to complete information on the project and equips them to monitor it. What further strengthens the process is that community

Box 3.11

Sharing Project Information Innovatively: Maharashtra Rural Water and Sanitation (Jalswarajya) Project

The Maharashtra Jalswarajya project has adopted a unique method for broad-basing project information. Instead of using a standard package of IEC (information, education and communication) practices for all project villages, the project created a small untied fund and placed it at the discretion of the *gram panchayat*, encouraging them to come up with ideas for awareness building appropriate to the local socio-cultural situation. This initiative from the project resulted in emergence of hundreds of innovative approaches in awareness building, each one of them unique in its own context! These have resulted into better performance of the fund earmarked for IEC, and better ownership of the project among the target community. It has also been instrumental in building the confidence of the *gram panchayat* to manage sub-projects, which will be implemented through them.

representatives are trained on construction aspects on a regular basis, and are supported by quality assurance manuals, which are developed in the local language and in simple, pictorial format. There have been occasions where the community stopped the work, as the contractors brought the equipment into the village during night time, and started the work before the community representatives had a chance to inspect the material.

3.4.2 Building the Capacities of the CBOs to Perform their Project Functions

In CDD projects, the CBOs need to be well-equipped to perform a variety of tasks, ranging from dealing with government departments, managing operation and maintenance of community infrastructure, resolving conflicts, etc. And the implementing agencies need to provide community members with knowledge and information useful to undertake these tasks. Specifically, CDD projects need to provide support to CBOs in terms of (a) building their technical, managerial and accounting skills required for decision making and implementation of project activities, and (b) provide information support to them on a continuous basis.

3.5 Strategy 5: Identify, Track and Act upon Unforeseen Project Issues

For most CDD projects, key performance questions are defined at the design stage, based on which indicators are identified and tracked throughout the project period. However there are two kinds of issues that either do not receive the required attention or get missed out completely. These are:

- Qualitative or process-related issues, which are typically not covered adequately in quantitative, progress related indicators that are developed at project design.
- Unintended or unexpected issues, which cannot be foreseen during the design stages and come up only during implementation.

Dealing with such issues involves identifying them, tracking or monitoring them and addressing them through a process of community-based learning.

Step 1. Identify critical project aspects that need to be monitored

Such issues can be identified using a variety of mechanisms, such as informal community level discussions, as well as more formal forums such as process monitoring exercises.

Identifying critical issues through a satellite based monitoring system

Jal Nirmal, a World Bank assisted rural water supply and sanitation project, is being implemented in 1758 villages of 11 districts of northern Karnataka. The project has adopted a unique mechanism for monitoring of project issues: satellite based programmes. The project makes use of the extensive satellite networks that the state government has set up for its other programmes. The programme follows a simple format that the community representatives and the project staff are familiar with.

- At each field office, which has a receiver and a television, the field staff invites 2-3 community groups at a designated time.
- The programme starts with the Project Director giving a brief on the project, which the villagers can watch on the TV sets, after which the transmission is switched off.
- This is followed by focus group discussions (FGDs) facilitated by the field staff, and raising issues of concern regarding the project that the community has.
- After the FGDs have been completed, the transmission is resumed, and the identified issues are taken up with the Project Director.
- The issues identified at these satellite programmes are followed up with the project staff through the regular monthly staff meetings.

The system helps the project staff, especially the top management, to get direct feedback from the community on various aspects of the project, and identify critical issues that need to be tracked. As a number of *taluka* offices are online at the same time, it is a learning experience for the community, and is also a forum for identifying best practices.

Identification and selection of issues for tracking can be tricky in project situations, when people have conflicting priorities and compulsions, and varying expectations from monitoring. Some lessons for selection of issues and the order in which they should be taken up for addressing:

Box 3.12

Capacity Building for Community Contracting: Swajal Project, India

The World Bank supported Swajal project in Uttar Pradesh, a rural water supply and environmental sanitation development project, adopted a community contracting model. Important decisions, such as technology choice, management of investment funds and contracting of goods, works and services, were made by the community, by the Village Water and Sanitation Committee (VWSC). In order that the VWSC is able to perform its functions effectively, the project consciously built its capacity in many ways:

- Training sessions on community contracting procedures for VWSCs were arranged in villages.
- Before the signing of the key Implementation Phase Tripartite Agreement, the support organisation organised a two-day training programme in the village for the VWSC to explain the details of the agreement and the roles and responsibilities of each signing party.
- Engineers of the project management unit (PMU) and the support organisation helped the Village Purchase Committee choose suitable materials and select good contractors to execute large works.
- Cross-visits were arranged for committee members to other project villages to show them how different groups are handling community contracting.

In order to increase the efficiency of community contracting, the PMU provides regular information on material procured by VWSCs; updated market rates of materials and works; rates of materials according to approved engineering designs and those actually procured by VWSCs, and information on innovative, efficient and cost effective practices followed by project village committees.

- Non-threatening issues: Many a time the issues are sensitive and perceived to be threatening to the project staff, as these would expose lapses on their part or on the part of the system. Under such circumstances, it is better to postpone handling such issues until the administration has more confidence and faith in the LME system.
- Picking up ripe issues: In some cases, the staff may not be convinced or for some reason, unwilling to take up the matter seriously. Under such circumstances, there is a need to generate additional data and convince a critical mass of officers before the issue can be addressed in a formal forum.
- Convergence of issue between top management and grassroots level: Issues that are perceived to be critical both at the top management level as well as at the grassroots level should be given priority.

Step 2. Identify 'monitorable' indicators in consultation with stakeholders

Given an opportunity, the community can come up with good performance and impact indicators. These may, at times, be at variance from those decided by the implementing agency, but certainly provide a different perspective on critical issues. For project managers, it is important to be open to such variations in perceptions of the community and integrate them in the monitoring systems, to the extent possible without compromising on the credibility of the information generated from the process.

Step 3. Gather and analyse data

There are a large number of tools and techniques available that can be utilised for gathering data.[3] These can be categorised as:

- PRA and PRA related tools (visual analysis, interviewing and sampling methods, group and team dynamics methods),
- Audio visual tools (use of videos, story-telling, popular theatre, songs etc.),
- Quantitative tools, and
- GIS (Geographical Information System) based tools.

It is often necessary to combine a number of methods. The complexity of data collection method and the staff capacity are important determinants of who is to collect, compile and analyse information. In general, higher the involvement of the intended users

Box 3.13

While Identifying Indicators

- **Be realistic. Don't set too many indicators. Think about the existing workload of staff, the financial resources and the staff available to carry out information collection and analysis.**
- **Choose the most important indicators. Limit their number so that you collect only the information you need most to answer your evaluation questions.**

3. The ASA PML experiment developed and used a number of participatory tools for PML, which have been documented in the form of a toolkit (complete reference at the end of chapter).

of the information in selecting the data collection methods, the chances that they will understand and use them correctly is higher (IFAD, 2002).

Step 4. Share LME learning periodically through institutional forums

Convincingly and credibly presenting the LME findings at different levels within the project management is perhaps the most challenging step in dealing with unforeseen issues.

- At the level of the World Bank, it can occur informally through interactions between the Bank task teams and the project managers. Other existing forums are the annual/six monthly reviews which include a supervision visit to the project, and the mid-term review.
- At the level of the borrower, information sharing and learning can be encouraged at the monthly review meetings at the district and state project units.

There are two guiding principles in deciding how to share findings with various project stakeholders:

Make sure that the findings are positioned in the context of information needs of stakeholders

There are multiple layers of decision makers within an organisation, each having varied information needs. No matter how critical the issue is, the information must be projected appropriately and in light of the specific needs at different levels. Make sure that

- At the field level, the findings are helpful in enhancing the operational efficiency of project staff, including troubleshooting.

In DPIP Madhya Pradesh, the ASA initiative was able to get a buy-in at the district level, only when the district level agencies including the project facilitating teams (PFTs) realised that it helped them resolve many of the operational problems that they were facing (high and increasing workloads, how to meet targets and how to monitor CIGs) and improving the efficiency of their operations (see case study in section III).

- At higher project management levels, findings are positioned in the context of the organisational policies and project strategies.

At project management levels, it is more important to present LME findings, backed by credible data and avoid generalisations based on a single or a few observations. Given the macro perspective of officers at the state headquarters

Box 3.14

Selecting the Right Data Gathering Tools and Techniques

- Make sure you explain to people collecting information why they are doing it and how it will be used.
- The tools and techniques selected should
  - be perceived by the community as a way to help them address their issues and problems, not merely as a means for external evaluators to collect information from them.
  - involve the community in generating and analysing data.
  - yield results that are reliable. Even if not quantitative, the results must be credible enough to convince decision makers.
  - be consistent in terms of complexity and cost involved to match the level of evaluation called for.
  - be gender sensitive.

level, it is necessary to develop a macro context around the issue before it can be discussed.

Use appropriate means to share information

Information disseminated in a written form may not always be appropriate for all kind of audiences, especially for reaching local audiences. Many projects have used innovative mechanisms for sharing information and encouraging critical learning. When sharing information with the communities, pictorial and audio-visual methods like wall paintings, street plays, etc. have been used effectively by many projects. Some examples of innovative means to share findings are as follows:

Box 3.15

Information Needs of Project Stakeholder

Community–learn from success, failure of local interventions—improve results.

NGOs/implementation arms of the project– what works and what doesn't—improve field level inputs/strategies.

Project management–overall performance in terms of outputs, outcomes and impacts—improve project level strategies.

Other stakeholders– Project impact on their stake, lessons on what works and what does not—what and how to contribute.

Donor–when to intervene—donor support strategies.

- The Jal Nirmal project in Karnataka has utilised the traditional system of *Jathas* (community street plays) effectively. Starting with introductory activities, which includes cleaning the village temple premises and the drinking water sources, the *Jatha* group talks about a range of issues including accessibility of water, sanitation facilities, water quality, health issues etc., in the process, educating the villagers on water related issues and earn their confidence. The team also presents street plays, magic shows, mime, songs, dance drama and folk arts, all with messages on water and sanitation. The cultural presentation speaks on the importance of water, safe-guarding water resources, need for safe drinking water, personal hygiene, cleanliness of the village, need for toilets and the role of the village community in all these issues. Once the show is over, the artists step out of characters and take stock of the success of the day's activities. They conduct a survey on the toilet facilities in each house. The team consolidates the findings of the survey, hands it over to the community facilitator and rests for the day, only to begin the same exercise next morning in the next village. The uniqueness of the *Jatha* is that the members are not merely artists but the agents of change who become a part of the village in the process of information dissemination.
- Complex tools such as GIS can be used for information sharing. Antrix, the external monitoring agency for Sujala Watershed Project in Karnataka uses GIS maps at community level meetings to pictorially depict trends in land-based parameters.

Step 5. Ensure that LME findings are integrated into the decision making process

One of the problems with the type of qualitative information that is often generated is that no definite mechanisms are put in place for its communication and it is left to the discretion of the project staff on whether to act on it or not. When analysis of such information is fed back to the project agency and the community, it is important to set in place mechanisms to track how this information influences decisions at various levels.

3.6 Strategy 6: Use Process Monitoring as a Management Tool during Project Implementation

Process monitoring (PM) is increasingly being used a management tool within projects, making them more participatory and demand responsive. This section presents some lessons from successful use of process monitoring, which can be used for CDD projects.

Process Monitoring is a continuous process of observation, interpretation, and institutional learning within a project. Process monitoring

- facilitates continuous assessment of how well the processes, procedures and criteria of a project are working, and
- provides timely feedback to decision-makers for change.

It involves participant observation and critical assessment. Process monitoring informs project management of the nature of changes needed to improve project responsiveness to community demands, maximise impact and improve the likelihood of sustainable outcomes. The success of process monitoring, however, depends to a very large extent on the willingness of the project management to change. Project staff, and in particular the project management, have to have an open mind to critical feedback for the process monitoring to achieve what it is supposed to. The following figure indicates how looking at 'processes' can differ from conventional M&E in the context of the Community Infrastructure Project, Pakistan (for details, see case study in section III); the rectangles indicate what the M&E/MIS system measures, and what process monitoring can provide, for one of the project steps selection of sub-project.

> **In general, monitoring information should help project staff perform better on the parameters they are appraised on.**

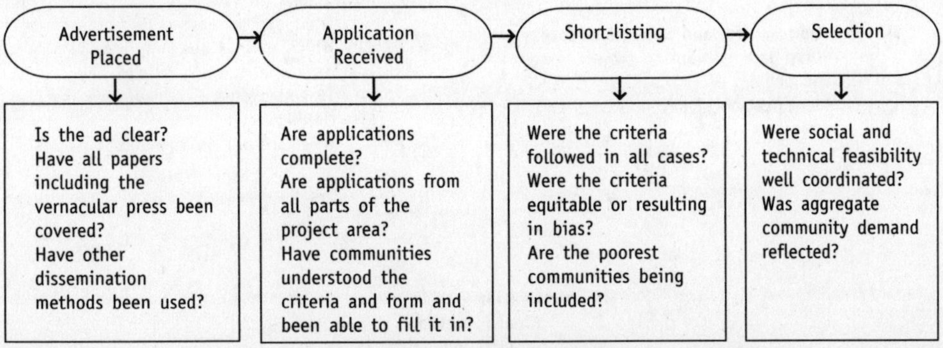

Process monitoring has been successfully implemented in a number of CDD projects, some of these experiences are discussed in detail in chapter 4. Typically, an independent agency is hired to lead the task and is assigned ToR for issues to monitor. Choice of issues is guided by information needs of senior management on factors considered critical for achievement of project development outcomes. Field researchers undertake documentation of organisational processes related to project implementation from the perspective of different stakeholders and this is presented to multiple stakeholder forums created at the field, middle management and top management levels. Feedback received from different stakeholders at each of these multiple stakeholder meetings is incorporated into decision making at each of these levels.

This section draws critical lessons from these and other CDD projects in the India portfolio that were reviewed for this guidebook, and makes suggestions on good practices in conducting process monitoring. Some of the common features that run through all these experiences are as follows:

- Establishing credibility among project stakeholders

Credibility amongst the stakeholders is a primary prerequisite for any third party to be involved in an activity as sensitive as process monitoring. The project agency must ensure that the communities as well as the project staff understand the relevance of process monitoring. Unless the pros and cons are fully explained and understood, the exercise may be perceived as intrusive and akin to policing

Figure 3.2

Steps Involved in Implementing Process Monitoring

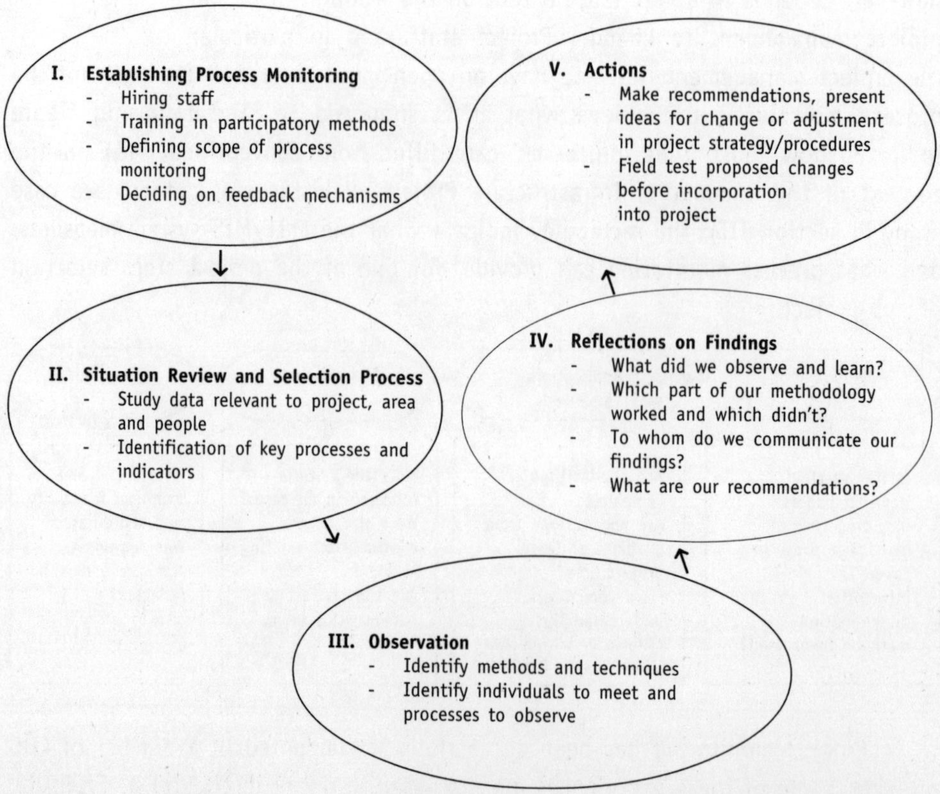

Source: CIP-SDC, 1999.

later. In most CDD projects, motivating the community to own a project is an implicit objective, and both direct and indirect measures are adopted to this end. It is important to extend the same effort towards increasing the buy-in and willingness to invest time towards the concept of process monitoring as well (refer to Sujala case study, discussed in chapter 4). Credibility may be built over time as and when the process monitoring information is found useful by the project. After the PM team faced stiff opposition from within the project, in the mid-term review of the CIP (Community Infrastructure Project, Pakistan, discussed in section III), the government specifically requested the continuation of the process monitoring activity, through to the close of the project!

- Involving project stakeholders in the process.

Open discussion on process monitoring findings at the field level is useful, before it is reported at the higher levels. When carried out in a collaborative, problem solving mode, this gives the field level functionaries a chance to explain the findings to the process monitoring team, as well as exploration of solutions in a collaborative manner.

- Establishing effective feedback loops and compliance systems.

A common element in all projects reviewed, where process monitoring has been used effectively, has been a clear compliance system. Action taken reports are a commonly used means.

- Support from the top management.

The attitude of the top management towards PM plays a key role in its acceptance and usage. It requires astute leadership for PM to be effective within a project setup, leadership that is objective in making judgements or reaching conclusions based on the information that the process monitoring exercise threw up. In the projects reviewed, change in top leadership led to considerable change in priorities at senior management level which were conveyed to the process monitoring agencies to varying extents in the two cases. Thus what was originally seen as very valuable information made available by the process monitoring exercise, now appeared as 'excessively critical conclusions of the process monitoring agency that did not take into account project priorities'.

Further reading:

Abbot, J. and I. Guijt (1998). "Changing Views on Change: Participatory Approaches to Monitoring the Environment", *Sustainable Agriculture and Rural Livelihoods Discussion Paper,* Number 2. UK: IIED.

ASA (2004). *A Handbook on Participatory Monitoring and Learning Tools,* Bhopal: Action for Social Advancement (ASA).

Botchway, Karl (2001). "Paradox of Empowerment: Reflections on a Case Study from Northern Ghana", *World Development,* 29(1), pp. 135-53.

CORE (2004). *Participatory Monitoring and Evaluation of Community and Faith Based Programmes: A Step By Step Guide For People Who Want To Make HIV And AIDS Services And Activities More Effective In Their Community,* Prototype version for field testing, November, The CORE Initiative, Washington DC, USA.

Estrella, Marisol and John Gaventa (19970. "Who Counts Reality? Participatory Monitoring and Evaluation: A Literature Review", *Working Paper* 70, Institute of Development Studies (IDS), available from, *http://www.ids.ac.uk/ids/bookshop/wp/wp70.pdf.*

FAO (1990). *Participatory Mentoring and Evaluation: A Handbook for Training Field Workers,* Bangkok: FAO.

Hogger, R. C., A. Kuchli, A. Zimmerman and E. Vokral (1997). *Monitoring: Keeping In Touch With Reality,* Swiss Agency for Development and Cooperation, *http://www.gtz.de/pcm/download/english/monit_e.pdf.*

IFAD (2002). *A Guide for Project M&E: Managing for Impact in Rural Development,* International Fund for Agricultural Development.

Vasan, Sudha (2002). "Ethnography of the Forest Guard: Contrasting Discourses, Conflicting Roles and Policy Implementation", *Economic and Political Weekly,* October.

World Bank (2002). *Sleeping On Our Own Mats: An Introductory Guide to Community Based Monitoring and Evaluation,* World Bank Rural Development- Africa region.

Websites

http://www.mande.co.uk

http://www.ids.ac.uk/eldis/hot/pme.htm

http://www.worldbank.org/participation/partme1.htm

Section III

Case Studies on Application of Learning-based M&E System

Chapter 4

Achieving Better Project Outcomes through a Learning-based M&E Systems

This chapter documents six case studies from World Bank supported projects, which have successfully used a learning-based M&E system for improving project outcomes. These are:

- Kecamatan Development Project (KDP), Indonesia;
- Community Infrastructure Project (CIP), Pakistan;
- Kerala Rural Water Supply and Sanitation Programme (KRWSS), India;
- Sujala Watershed Project, Karnataka, India;
- District Poverty Initiatives Project (DPIP), Andhra Pradesh, India;
- District Poverty Initiatives Project (DPIP), Madhya Pradesh, India.

The case study projects are drawn from different sectors ranging from poverty alleviation, infrastructure, and watershed development. They are widely divergent in terms of socio-cultural, economic and political contexts as well as scale. The KDP project of Indonesia stands out in terms of its scale of operations. While all the projects are community-driven, KDP and DPIP were specifically targeted to the poor. DPIP in both the states, Andhra Pradesh and Madhya Pradesh, were implemented through autonomous institutions promoted by the state and therefore had a more open and less bureaucratic organisational culture as compared to the others, which were all implemented by government departments or ministries. Both DPIPs have achieved organisational learning although there are significant differences in their approaches. In the first case, (AP-DPIP) a system of process documentation has been institutionalised and integrated into the M&E of the project right from inception. In the case of MP-DPIP, an attempt was made to create a learning forum at the grassroots which generates valuable feedback for different stakeholders and for different levels in the implementing organisation. In both the cases external agencies are involved in initiating the learning activities.

A critical difference in these projects is the scale of application of the learning-based M&E system itself. The M&E system of the Kecamatan Development Project in Indonesia was developed systematically at the beginning of the project, while the process-monitoring component of the Community Infrastructure Project in Pakistan evolved over time. At the other end of the spectrum is DPIP-Madhya Pradesh, in which participatory monitoring was introduced as a pilot project midway through the project and was experimented with for almost two years. What runs as a common thread in all the case studies is use of learning-based M&E system for guiding project strategy and a continued emphasis on organisational learning.

4.1 Integrating Participatory Monitoring within the M&E System in a Large CDD Project: The Kecamatan Development Project (KDP), Indonesia

The KDP in Indonesia is one of the largest World Bank-financed CDD projects, with a budget of about $700 million for its first two phases (1998 to 2006). KDP's goals are to alleviate poverty by raising rural incomes and providing increased economic opportunities at the village level, strengthen local government and community institutions, and build public infrastructure. The KDP gives power to communities by placing funds and the planning and decision making processes directly in the hands of villagers. It provides block grants directly to Kecamatan[1] and villages for small-scale infrastructure, social, and economic activities. Starting from a small pilot operation in 25 villages in 1997, KDP grew to cover more than 28,000 villages in 2003.

4.1.1 *The KDP M&E System*

During its first phase (1998-2002), KDP developed an extensive M&E system to track the progress and evaluate its impact, using the following steps:

1. Review all the project documentation to understand fully the project background.
2. Meet with key stakeholders to understand their information needs.
3. Determine the key questions and issues for the M&E system.
4. Develop indicators that are measurable, relevant and gender-disaggregated, when possible.
5. Determine means of verification or tools to collect the information for the indicators.
6. Decide who is responsible for collecting that information.

Box 4.1

M&E Components of KDP

Internal Monitoring:

- Reporting by government officials and field consultants
- Community participatory monitoring
- Case studies and documentation of lessons
- Financial supervision and training
- Handling complaints and grievance procedures

External Monitoring:

- NGO independent monitoring
- Independent journalists' monitoring

Evaluation:

- Impact evaluation study
- Technical infrastructure and economic activities evaluations
- Audits and financial reviews
- World Bank supervision missions

1. Kecamatan are Indonesian sub-districts containing on average 20 to 25 villages with a population of some 60,000 persons.

7. Determine the approximate time frame for collecting the information.

8. Develop rough budget approximations for each activity.

9. Link the M&E information to decision-making forums and develop regular reporting flows.

10. Review periodically the M&E plan.

The system developed is a combination of quantitative and qualitative tools, including internal monitoring from programmes stakeholders and external independent monitoring by Indonesian non-governmental organisations (NGOs), journalists, and audit teams.

4.1.2 The Learning-based Monitoring and Evaluation System in KDP

Over the years, the KDP encouraged different kinds of community based monitoring systems:

Monitoring by Village Councils: The village councils have the responsibility of monitoring KDP activities at all stages: social mobilisation, planning, implementation, and maintenance. They select members to monitor each phase. Results of this monitoring are then discussed at council meetings and fed into larger village meetings.

Monitoring by Special Community Teams: Communities form special teams during the village meetings to monitor KDP. These community monitoring groups are independent of the village implementation teams, similar to the social audit teams being promoted under some CDD projects. The community team members share responsibilities for checking financial accounts, monitoring bank transactions and material purchases, visiting suppliers to confirm the costs of goods, and monitoring sub-project activities, including infrastructure construction.

Community Participatory Monitoring Facilitated by NGOs: NGOs help a number of villages, special groups and teams conduct community participatory monitoring. They help villagers decide what questions were important to them about KDP, how to collect data to answer these questions, and helped villagers analyse community findings.

Handling Complaints and Grievances: Complaints and questions about KDP can be directed to any KDP field consultant or government official. Complaints can also be sent to a special post office box in Jakarta and the KDP national project secretariat office. Project brochures and posters include information on where to send complaints. Special staff has been recruited who are specifically responsible for ensuring that complaints are addressed and investigated as required in the field. The complaints and grievances are entered into a centralised database, which make it possible to track the status of complaints. It has also proved to be a useful repertoire of project knowledge. As of July 2002, 1,900 problems or complaints had been reported—an average of 45 per month—of which 49 per cent had been resolved and 51 per cent were still in process.

Additionally, the following learning mechanisms have been used by the project:

- KDP received regular monthly reports from field consultants, which provided useful information on problems in the field and what needed to be followed up by the proper parties. Additional information on the monthly reporting system is presented in Annexure A-5.
- Another source of learning for the project was tracking newspaper reports. It was ensured that problems described in those reports were communicated to field staff and government officials for follow-up.

4.1.3 Usefulness of the KDP LME System

The KDP model is regarded as extremely successful. KDP's bottom-up planning produces significantly lowered costs and achieved better rates of return than standard project approaches do. *Ex post* review of KDP sub-projects showed them costing about 25 per cent less than the next cheapest form of infrastructure construction and as much as 50 per cent less than normal public works budgets for the same items. Within Indonesia, KDP's fundamental design is being scaled up and the model is now spreading *horizontally* to primary education, health, and natural resource management, with similarly positive results.

The M&E system, especially the participatory monitoring mechanisms, played a critical role in this success. In order to ensure constant flow of feedback, it relied on multiple methods and multiple sources of information. The inclusion of external stakeholders such as consultants and journalists for regular monitoring of the project was a special feature that helped to make operations transparent and make the bureaucracy and the CBOs more accountable. The findings provided information for programme managers to take corrective action and adjust project procedures during the course of the project. Regular tracking of complaints helped improve accountability of project staff.

4.1.4 Key Messages from the KDP LME System

- Ensure that the scope of M&E system is in line with the resources available.

The establishment of the KDP M&E system would not have been possible if the World Bank and the Indonesian government had not committed financial and technical resources towards this effort. M&E activities (along with budget allocations) such as journalist monitoring, special studies, and complaint-handling procedures were incorporated into the Project Appraisal Document and Loan Agreement.

- Ensure that there is a direct link between M&E findings and actions taken.

In KDP, this was evidenced in several tangible ways: the handling of grievances and complaints; suspension of activities in problem areas; reformulation of procedures for each project year; and the incorporation of lessons and best practices for the design of KDP phase two. The NGOs were required to provide oral and written reports at the monthly coordination meetings for consultants and provincial and district government coordination teams. Majority of provinces incorporated the NGO reports and recommendations into their monthly meetings and action plans.

- Combine quantitative instruments with qualitative research in a complementary manner.

The methodology combined quantitative instruments (household surveys, regular monthly field reporting) with qualitative research (case studies). It supported participatory methods such as community participatory monitoring along with more highly specialised monitoring and evaluation activities such as financial audits and sector studies.

- Use internal and external monitoring in a complementary manner.

In order to provide a wide array of perspectives as well as cross-triangulation of data, KDP incorporated both internal and external monitoring. It identified who are the best stakeholders to undertake monitoring activities, and engaged them in a complementary manner. It took advantage of NGOs' skills in community development and knowledge of local situation and contracted them in each province to monitor KDP's progress. NGO findings were cross-checked and validated against those of KDP's internal monitoring system. Journalists were able to adhere to the principles of independent, unbiased journalism in covering KDP activities and were not subject to outside intervention or censorship that would affect their reporting. In several provinces, the newspaper articles had a direct impact on policy makers by pressuring them to take action.

- Decentralise monitoring functions to minimise response time on M&E findings.

Based on lessons from KDP1, KDP2 decentralised the handling of complaints. There are complaints officer in each region, which should improve communications with provincial and district government coordination teams and resolve grievances more expeditiously.

- Build the capacities of the monitoring agencies.

Evaluations of KDP1 revealed that NGOs involved in monitoring need to have a deep understanding of how KDP works and its procedures, their reports were sometimes late or unclear and coordination between NGOs, consultants, and provincial coordination teams could be improved. Similarly, the consultants involved in handling complaints need more training in dispute resolution. In view of this, KDP2 emphasises capacity building of the monitoring agencies, especially to improve the skills of communities and consultants in technical supervision, financial oversight, and contracting.

4.2 Process Monitoring for Making Course Corrections: Community Infrastructure Project (CIP), Pakistan

The Community Infrastructure Project (CIP) was implemented in the NWFP (North Western Frontier Province) of Pakistan between 1996 and 2003. The CIP involved infrastructure upgrading in the areas of water supply, sanitation/drainage, access roads, solid waste management for rural and urban low income communities. The project was implemented by the Local Government, Elections and Rural Development Department (LGE&RD), and involved infrastructure upgrading for 90 rural and urban low income communities, reaching 550,000 (direct) and over 600,000 (direct and indirect) beneficiaries. The community was required to contribute 20 per cent of cost of community works.

Box 4.2

Initiating Process Monitoring: The Path of Most Resistance!

The initial response to process monitoring was not a positive one. Perceived as an externally imposed, additional burden, the process monitoring team was initially accused of 'spying' for the donors, and of adding little value to the traditional M&E system. Where expectations of revolutionary differences were not met, it was difficult initially to achieve 'buy-in' to this innovative activity. Since many of the indicators of 'process' were similar to indicators of progress or impact, this led to initial confusion and scepticism.

***Source*: Viloria and Hosain.**

4.2.1 Setting up of the Process Monitoring System

The Process Monitoring (PM) team, administered by World Bank-Water & Sanitation Program (WSP), was set up to generate learning for project processes which were innovative in nature. The group faced a lot of opposition when it was initiated. A fundamental problem was a lack of clarity among the stakeholders to understand the 'difference' between 'Process Monitoring' and other forms of M&E. Over time however, as the value of process information began to filter through to project management, they began to increasingly request studies to analyse bottlenecks, issues and best practices. Communities used the process monitoring 'platform' to analyse key issues, reflect on the effectiveness of their own organisations, and channel feedback to project management to influence decision making. At every level, process monitoring looked not only at whether the process is being carried out correctly, but also at the relevance and appropriateness of the process in meeting core objectives. Case studies and field reports, combined with visual documentation and the setting up of a 'Process Monitoring Working Group' forum, which brought together all levels of staff, including field staff along with the PMT: all provided a major vehicle for disseminating the PM learnings.

4.2.2 Effectiveness of the Process Monitoring System

The presence of process monitoring continuously shifted the focus from the achievement of physical and financial targets, towards the quality of community outreach and capacity building, towards issues of transparency and governance, and towards the core development objectives of the project. Where community mobilisation and development process had once been viewed as a mere formality and even a hurdle to reach physical implementation, it now became the key area of attention.

Box 4.3

High Dropout Rate: An Issue Identified by Process Monitoring

An important issue, which emerged early in the project, was that a surprisingly high number of communities were dropping out during the course of sub-project selection. The management tended to see the problem as one of failure to meet technical and financial feasibility criteria, scattered settlement patterns and poor coordination between line departments who were supposed to plan and deliver services.

But was this the whole story? Why were so many communities failing to meet selection criteria? Process documentation analysed this issue and brought to light the following reasons for this:

- Lack of coordination between the social and technical wings of the project.
- Lengthy, bureaucratic procedures that which resulted in loss of the community's interest and confidence in the project.
- Lack of clarity of project rules and the communication of these rules to both Project staff and community members.

The PMT brought these issues to the notice of the project management, who then took concrete corrective steps.

Key areas where changes resulted in the project cycle and its processes through process monitoring are as follows:

Sub-Project Cycle Stage	*Issue Identified by Process Monitoring*	*Decision Taken*
Sub-Project Identification	Efforts to disseminate project information were limited.	Clear and widely disseminated advertisements, supported with mass meetings and other forms of dissemination.
	High rate of community dropout at this stage, resulting largely from poor coordination between departments, which delayed the process, leading to a loss of interest in the community.	Coordination between social and technical staff to determine feasibility improved. Coordination between line agencies ensured to prevent duplication of work.
Sub-Project Preparation	Formal surveys did not accurately convey community needs, and the needs of women were being ignored.	Participatory methodologies introduced.
	Community development staff was spending much of their time on largely irrelevant data collection.	Data collection has been rationalised. Time of community development staff focused on building community contact.
	Women's participation was minimal. There was token representation on male committees, where women never appear physically.	Women's participation ensured through setting up separate organisations. Special women's 'programmes' formulated to improve participation.
Confirmation and Implementation	Long periods without contact with the project communities and lengthy were destroying community trust in the department.	The communities are kept informed and continuous contact is maintained with them.
	Changes were being made in planned infrastructure development without consultation with the community.	Systems have been put in place to ensure that communities are involved at all stages of survey and design finalisation.
	Slow progress on sub-project implementation.	Implementation bottlenecks such as contractor rates, and government contracting in certain types of works analysed.
	Front-line field staff was completely marginalised.	Setting up of a Process Monitoring Working 'Group' brought them into decision-making.

4.2.3 Key Messages

What distinguishes the CIP's process monitoring system, and has succeeded in leveraging change, are the following features:

- Continuous participation of the process monitoring team.

The constant presence of a team which continuously participated in all key processes at all levels, observed them, added a continuity, depth and accuracy to the data generated, which can never be found in regular, quantitative monitoring or *ex-post* monitoring or evaluation. The team is perceived as a 'participant', and has access to information and dynamics, which would not otherwise be forthcoming.

- Working with others.

The PMT needs to invest considerable time at the beginning to develop a positive working relationship with all project units. The PMT in CIP built and expanded its links with other project units through Working Group meetings, monthly planning and progress review meetings and joint field visits.

- An 'internal-external' arrangement.

The process monitoring team was set up by the World Bank-WSP midway through the project. Process monitoring draws on the M&E/MIS data generated to identify bottlenecks and analyse issues, and feeds information on issues of quality to the M&E system. The PMT is an integral part of the M&E system, with specific staff (one female and one male) assigned to the activity, and reporting directly to the Director General. 'External' accountability allowed the PMT to be independent and objective in their findings and analysis, without buckling under management pressure to gloss over facts. At the same time they were seen as 'neutral' and enjoyed the confidence of project staff and other stakeholders. This is a critical element of good 'process monitoring', which should not ideally be totally internalised.

- Effective feedback loops.

The 'Process Monitoring Working Group' provided an effective forum to feedback findings to senior management, and translate them to 'process changes'. This Working Group also gave field staff a voice in decision making they had never had. The routine monitoring reports at various levels were generated and shared within the respective levels i.e. PMU (project management unit) and government/donors for their information and decision making. The M&E outputs were also used by LGE&RDD during the monthly/quarterly review meetings by the Project Review Board for overall project review and policy making. In addition, the M&E unit became a knowledge bank for community approaches, and information is shared with other organisations as well.

The ultimate test of the success of process monitoring is whether the information it generates leads to concrete decisions and actions to address critical issues to improve project performance.

4.3 Community-based Monitoring: Kerala Rural Water Supply and Sanitation Programme, India

The Kerala Rural Water Supply and Sanitation (KRWSS) Programme or Jalanidhi was launched in 1999 as a pilot project. It aims to assist Government of Kerala in improving the quality of rural water supply and environmental sanitation service delivery. The project, currently in its implementation phase, is expected to cover 80 to 100 *gram panchayats* (GPs) by the year 2006. The project is a demand driven one, where groups of households form a cluster (a beneficiary group, or a BG) and apply for a drinking water scheme. The community investment funds are routed through the GPs, who are responsible for the execution of the project and required to make a financial contribution to the tune of 10 per cent of the project cost, in addition to the 15 per cent contributed by the BG.

Jalanidhi is a project where the community plays a key role in monitoring the project processes; in fact they are responsible for steering it completely. Some of the mechanisms that help the process are:

- Agree-to-participate meeting, which is held before a BG is registered. This meeting is facilitated by the project agency to obtain public commitment from the BG.
- Agree-to-do meeting, where technical alternatives are presented by the project implementation agency to the BG and discussed.
- Agree-to-implement meeting, where the various modalities, including the responsibilities of the three parties involved, the BG, the GP and the implementing agency are worked out.

Box 4.5

Gram Panchayat as a Project Monitoring Agency

The gram *panchayat* plays a key role in the project monitoring. It ratifies all payments and expenditures made by the BGs. It is one of the signatories of the various agreements: the PITA (Planning, Implementation Tripartite Agreement) between the SO (support organisation, a local NGO hired by the GP as service provider), the GP, the BG, and the IPQA (Implementation Phase Quadrilateral Agreement) between the Implementing agency, the GP, the BG and the SO. What makes this high level of decentralisation possible within the project and stimulates the GPs to take an active interest in monitoring are:

- The GPs in the state are very active, used to handling large budgets, dealing with government officials and resolving most problems at the local level itself. For most, this project is another activity in the huge portfolio of activities that they are already handling, and this lends a certain degree of professionalism and efficiency in operations.
- This is one of the few projects where the SO, typically an NGO, is selected by and is accountable to the GP directly and not the project implementing agency.
- The education and political awareness level is very high in the state. The presence of strong opposition at the GP level also contributes to the high quality performance by the political parties ruling the GP.

4.3.1 The LME System of Jalanidhi

- Progress monitoring.
- Process monitoring: (a) quantitative, through structured routine reporting on BGs, self-assessment by BGs and sample evaluation studies. BGs and *gram panchayats* also carry out social audits at regular intervals. (b) Qualitative: self-evaluation by all stakeholders.
- Monitoring outcomes and sustainability.

The learning-based monitoring system of Jalanidhi project is facilitated by an external agency, with complete community involvement. The external agency takes up process monitoring every six months.

4.3.1.1 Steps in Process Monitoring

1. The PM team identifies a sample of GPs and BGs, based on discussions with the KRWSS staff.
2. It makes preliminary visits to the sites and develops a methodology, which is reviewed by KRWSS monitoring and learning team.
3. Process monitoring is carried out using a set of participatory and quantitative methodologies including PRA methods (wealth ranking/ seasonality calendars), semi-structured surveys, data collection from sample households for detailed analysis, participant-observation in regular meetings, etc.
4. Based on the above analysis, the BGs are ranked.
5. The analysis is discussed with the district office and the PM team goes back to the BGs with low ranks, shares the findings with them and explores options to remedy the situation.

According to the KWRRS management, the composition of the PM team is very important for this approach to be successful. The team consists of a social scientist, who takes the lead in community interactions and a technical specialist, who provides the necessary technical backstopping in the process, to ensure that the community groups come up with appropriate technical solutions to the problems identified.

4.3.2 How Effective is Participatory Monitoring?

As of April 2005, 1261 water supply schemes, managed by 1304 BGs had been completed under Jalanidhi. The average maintenance cost of a water supply scheme is Rs. 39 per month per family. The production cost of water per kilo litre is Rs. 3.38 which is cheaper compared to other schemes. Currently, 768 schemes are at different stages of implementation, and more than 1800 new BGs have come forward and registered for taking up the Jalanidhi project.

The various community forums created under the project play a key role in broad-basing information on the project, demystifying technology-related issues and providing an opportunity to the community to clarify issues. Involving the community at the most decentralised level has meant that the project is very close to the primary stakeholders, with high involvement of users' in all aspects and there is a better chance of sustainability.

According to the project implementing agency, process monitoring has been providing feedback that enables the programme design to be improved continuously. Lessons learned from the early phases are being incorporated in subsequent ones. The process monitoring has been instrumental in effecting key policy changes in Jalanidhi.

- During the implementation phase of Jalanidhi, the PM team pointed out that once a project (and the SO) withdrew from an area, many of the older systems were becoming dysfunctional. Even when the BGs informed the SOs of the problem, the project did not have a budget for the SOs to go back to older project areas and undertake repair and maintenance work. Once this issue was identified and analysed, the project allocated funds for undertaking repair and maintenance work in older project areas, as and when the need arose.
- Earlier, the SOs were paid a lump sum amount, paid in equal installments during the planning and implementation phases. The process monitoring pointed out that a lump sum payment does not provide any incentive for efficiency. Additionally, as there is no uniformity in the geographical size of GPs, there is no justification for a uniform, lump sum payment. Acting on this finding, the project shifted to an output-based payment system, where the payment was broken down in line with the sub-activities of the project.

The GPs are normally very active and able to resolve the issues faced by the BGs. However, there are higher level issues that can be more effectively dealt with at a cluster of BGs level. Examples include delays in obtaining electricity connections, issues related to land required for the water scheme, and political issues. This was brought to the attention of the project and the solution that emerged was creating a federations of BGs that would provide support to individual BGs as well as take up common issues.

4.3.3 Key Messages

- The community and CBOs have an interest in monitoring the project performance only when they have decision making and financial powers.

The project funds in Jalanidhi are routed through the GPs, who make a financial contribution to the tune of 10 per cent of the project cost and are responsible for the execution of the project. The GPs thus have a stake in the project, and take an active interest in monitoring its performance.

- All stakeholders must have complete clarity on what their monitoring roles are, and be well trained to carry them out.

The planning and monitoring roles of the various stakeholders: BGs, GPs, SOs, etc. are clearly spelt out in the various project agreements. Through various forums, the project makes additional efforts to ensure that the functions are made adequately clear to all stakeholders. The BGs and the GPs are provided capacity building inputs throughout the sub-project cycle in order that they are able to perform their tasks effectively and efficiently. While the SOs are accountable to the GPs, the project supports the GPs in making their selection, as well as monitoring their performance.

4.4 Using Process Monitoring Effectively: Sujala Watershed Project, Karnataka, India

Sujala is a community-driven watershed development project implemented by the Watershed Development Department of Government of Karnataka state. Launched in 2001, the project is being implemented in 7 districts, covering 5.16 lakh hectares of land in 1270 villages, benefiting nearly 4 lakhs households. The project's development objective is to improve the productive potential of selected watersheds and their associated natural resource base, and strengthen community and institutional arrangements for natural resource management.

The monitoring, evaluation and learning (M,E&L) system is a central aspect of the project, and being carried out by an external agency, Antrix Corporation, a division of the Indian Space Research Organisation, Bangalore. This case study focuses on the process monitoring component of the M,E&L system of Sujala.

4.4.1 Process Monitoring in Sujala

During the initial phase of the project, in order to develop a strategy for process monitoring, Antrix organised a series of workshops with the field NGOs, the implementing arm of the project. At these workshops, each project activity was broken down into processes, and indicators developed to track them. This formed the basis for process monitoring.

Antrix carries out process monitoring through its staff at the district level. Each project district has 2-3 Antrix staff members, stationed at the district Sujala project office. Steps in undertaking PM are as follows:

- Representatives from the district M,E&L cell visit sample sub-watersheds every month, identify critical issues, and discuss the findings and feasible corrective actions with the field level staff. This is useful as it (a) helps the PM team understand the context of and get clarity on the issues; (b) makes the PM team a part of the collaborative problem-solving process; and (c) provides a forum for the project field staff to discuss their problems with the PM team, which eventually get recorded in the PM reports.
- The PM team submits monthly process monitoring reports to the M,E&L cell at the head office. The district implementing arm is required to submit compliance reports on each of the issues identified within a period of two months.
- The findings are discussed in the monthly audio conference between the field level functionaries and the head office.
- The assessment reports of the monthly process monitoring are presented by the district M,E&L staff at the monthly 'open house' meetings of the Executive Committees of the Sujala watersheds. These reports are discussed in detail, and actions and responsibilities on compliance decided.

4.4.2 How Effective is Process Monitoring in Sujala

According to the project implementing agency, inputs from process monitoring have been extremely useful in guiding project strategy. PM has brought to light issues like misappropriation of funds, inefficient functioning, because of which changes in the village level committees have been made. The process monitoring is also useful in identifying success stories, which are taken up for detailed documentation and shared as best practices throughout the project.

4.4.3 Key Messages

- Ensure that the project staff and the community understand the usefulness of PM.

The implementing agency took special measures to build the credibility of Antrix, the external monitoring agency, with the community. During the planning phase, along with awareness creation about the core components of the project, the project staff discussed the importance of process monitoring with the community. Wherever feasible, they also introduced the district M,E&L staff to the community, and included them in discussions. This was of great help, as (a) it helped Antrix to get a buy-in with the community, (b) it also gave them an opportunity to understand the project and its constituents well, as a result of which they were not regarded as policemen later.

- Build the capacity of the process monitoring team.

In Antrix, the entire M,E&L staff meets every month, which are also used to conduct training sessions on specific topics such as research methodologies, data analysis, facilitation skills, etc. In addition, Antrix organises six monthly workshops for its staff on special issues such as social inclusion, which are of importance to the project. The staff also undergoes a rigorous training in data collection, analysis before any thematic study is launched, which ensures the quality of output.

- Decentralise process monitoring functions.

Having M,E&L staff at the district office lends credibility to the process monitoring. For the district implementation teams, the Antrix team is always available for advice and discussions. While known to be objective, they are considered 'part of the team', and not outsiders who come in once in a while and critically comment on their work, with no accountability. Being close to the field, the Antrix district teams understand the ground situation better and report more responsibly.

4.5 Process Monitoring for Guiding Project Strategy: Andhra Pradesh DPIP, India

The Andhra Pradesh District Poverty Initiatives Project (AP-DPIP) was launched in 2000. The project tries to create livelihood security opportunities for the rural poor primarily through the instrument of self-help groups (SHGs) and common interest groups (CIGs), which are groups of poor people brought together by a common interest. It also builds the capacity of existing local institutions, especially the *gram panchayats*. The project is operating in 22 districts of the state, and aims to reach 29 lakhs of the poorest of rural poor. It is being implemented by the Society for Elimination of Rural Poverty (SERP), an independent, autonomous society registered under the Societies Act.

The monitoring and evaluation system of AP-DPIP has four distinct components: (a) input-output monitoring through computerised MIS; (b) tracking performance of project promoted community institutions; (c) process monitoring; and (d) baseline, mid term and end of project impact assessment. This case study focuses on the process-monitoring component of the M&E system and its contribution towards guiding project strategy. The process monitoring component is carried out by an external agency contracted by the project: a development NGO called Society for Human Rights and Social Development (SOCHURSOD).

4.5.1 Approach to Process Monitoring

In PM, each process or a set of inter-related processes associated with major interventions of the project is tracked at more than one level of the project. For most project processes, information is collected from four different levels:

- State Project Management Unit (SPMU),
- District Project Management Unit (DPMU),
- *Mandal* (sub-district) Community Support Cell (MCSC)/*Mandal Samakhya* (MS) and
- Village/community level.

However, the source of information and stakeholder(s) at each level is different. For example, information relating to social mobilisation needs to be collected at multiple levels. While policy relating to social mobilisation is collected from the SPMU, the details of implementation strategy are gathered from the DPMU. At the *mandal* level, views of the project frontline staff are collected while at the community level, the actual dynamics of mobilisation are observed.

Table 4.1

Sources/Levels of Information Collection for Process Monitoring in AP-DPIP

	SPMU/RPD Level	*District/DPMU Level*	*Mandal/MCSC Level*	*Village/Community Level*
Source	CEO, Addl. CEO, SPMs, RPDs	Project Director (PD), Asst. Project Director (APD), Dist. Project Manager (DPM), heads of select line departments, bankers, other partners (NGOs, etc.), resource persons, etc.	Asst. Project Manager (APM), Livelihood Assistant, Cluster Coordinator (CC), resource persons, Master book keepers, bankers, *Mandal Samakhya* (MS) members, President and members of *Mandal Parishads*	Village organisation/ SHGs/activists/para-professionals, CIF beneficiaries, *anganwadi* workers, teachers, *sarpanches*/members of *gram panchayat*, etc.

Process monitoring in AP-DPIP is conducted on a quarterly basis covering all the project districts.

4.5.2 Conducting Process Monitoring: Steps

- The process monitoring team (PMT) develops a schedule and gets it approved by the concerned DPMU.
- On reaching the district for a process monitoring round, the PMT meets the PD to understand the progress of the project during the reporting period, the district-specific processes to be covered in that particular round and the action taken on the observations of the earlier round of PM.
- The PMT members have one-to-one interactions with the DPMs. The purpose of those interactions is to have an understanding of the progress within the functional area, identify processes to be monitored and to know the action taken on the earlier observations. Care is taken to see that the same team member interacts with a particular DPM during each round. This is important in order to ensure continuity of processes and to follow up on the plans indicated during the earlier round of process monitoring.
- The PMT compiles a list of processes for monitoring in the field.
- The PMT covers these and the processes identified for monitoring on a regular basis during the next 3-4 days of the field visits. The methods adopted for process monitoring are mostly participatory and specific tools have been developed to cover different processes and all project components (Table 4.3).
- The observations at each level are analysed then and there and shared with the concerned group/individuals that are responsible to act on it.
- Each district level PM round ends with a debriefing session at the DPMU, with the PD and the DPMs. It is during this session that a list of 'agree to do' actions are arrived at, the completion of which is monitored during the consecutive round.
- On return from the district, the PMT prepares a detailed report for each round and submits it to the SPMU and the concerned DPMU. These reports include a discussion on processes tracked, an analysis of the progress based on MIS data, concerns/gaps and suggested actions.
- The PMT makes a presentation to the SPMU during the PDs conference once every six months and to the World Bank Supervision Mission during its visit.

In AP-DPIP, the institutions once selected for process monitoring are monitored for a continuous period of three years i.e., the PM team goes back to the same MSs, VOs and SHGs during the same quarter for two consecutive years. This is done to facilitate the assessment of institutional maturity over a period of time.

Table 4.2

Process Monitoring: Illustrative Methods and Tools

	Level		
SPMU	*District/DPMU*	*Mandal/ MS*	*VO/SHG/CIG*
• Semi-structured interviews (SSIs) • FGDs with functional units Perusal of : • progress reports - process documents - case studies - training registers - minutes of review meetings - special studies - inter-office communications	• SSIs • FGDs with functional staff Perusal of: - progress reports - process documents - case studies - training registers - minutes of review meetings - special studies - SP proposals, appraisal reports - reports sent to SPMU	• FGDs with MS • Observation of MS meetings • Individual interviews • PRA tools • Perusal of records maintained by MS, APM and CC • Stakeholder analysis (line deptts., DPIP staff, CBOs) • Quantitative tools	• FGDs with SHG/CIG/VO • Participant observation of SHG meetings • PM tools developed for DPIP (VOs/SHGs): - well being analysis - selection criterion matrix - time lines - process and decision making matrix - Venn diagrams • SHG assessment formats • Spider analysis to assess institutional maturity • Interviews with beneficiaries of SPs. • Household questionnaires • SHG and VO rating tools • Case studies • Perusal of secondary information-SHG registers, books of accounts, base line, etc.

4.5.3 Translating Learning into Action

Process monitoring within AP-DPIP has been instrumental in influencing decisions at various levels: operational as well as strategic. The following table provides information on the type of learning and action taken in response to that learning at three different levels *viz.* a) grassroots functionaries b) district level and c) state (project) level.

Table 4.3

Learning and Action Taken at Grassroots Functionaries' Level

Process Monitored	*Learning*	*Learning Type*	*Action Taken*
Participation in CBO	Regularity in conduct of meetings and attendance at meetings.	Single-loop	Groups committed to improving performance levels. Number of sample groups recorded improvement at the time of repeat visit.
Participation in CBO	Low involvement of VOs in the implementation of CIF-SPs.	Single-loop	A system of having sub-committees at the VO level has been introduced. Committees are responsible for various tasks related to the process of SP implementation.
Decision making in CBO	Savings deposited in banks by few SHGs. No practice of internal lending.	Single-loop	Issue discussed in the monthly meeting of the MS. All VOs advised to ensure SHGs practice internal lending. Facilitated understanding of the importance of internal lending in the rating scale.

The table shows that monitoring the processes of participation and decision making within the CBOs led to mid-course corrections which are in line with the expectations of the project. These are instances of single loop learning so far as the grassroots functionaries are concerned.

Table 4.4

Learning and Action at the District Level

Process Monitored	*Learning*	*Learning Type*	*Action taken*
Capacity Building of Staff	CCs found wanting in culturally-sensitive strategies.	Single-loop	CCs have been inducted into tribal, backward caste and other cultural sensitivities. Street plays have been organised and cultural coordinators/activists have been hired/appointed to facilitate the early rapport building processes.
Implementation Process	Inadequate convergence with District Rural Development Agency.	Double-loop learning	Convergence with DRDA has been clearly worked out; necessary Government Order issued. A total merger at the district level has taken place since then.
Implementation Process	Rapid project expansion leading to dilution of staff's efforts.	Double-loop learning	Decision taken on reorganisation of staff at the district and sub-district level. Guidelines issued for introduction of cluster (5-7 *mandals)* based system of project implementation.
Accountability of Grassroots Functionaries and Empowerment of People's Institutions	Systems to promote accountability of frontline staff not in place.	Single-loop learning	Review of staff and presentation of 'work done report' included as non-negotiable item of the agenda for the monthly EC meeting of the MS. EC members pay salaries only on being satisfied with the work.

At the district level, the learning led to identification of operational issues (SLL) as well as strategic issues (DLL). The DLL issues were concerned with the process of implementation *viz.* convergence with DRDA and decentralisation in order to cope with the speed and scale of implementation. A large number of SLL issues were to do with capacity building of staff. The issue of accountability is likely to have emerged at the village/community level and fed at the sub-district/ *Mandal Samakhya* (MS) level. A mature decision seems to have been taken in response to the feedback from lower levels.

Table 4.5

Learning and Action Taken at State (Project) Level

Process monitored	*Learning*	*Learning type*	*Action taken*
Recruitment	Lack of uniform methodology in the selection of CCs and SOs (APMs)	Single-loop learning	The recruitment of CCs/APMs has become systematic–desk scrutiny for the qualifications etc., written test and short-listing, 3-4 day village stay, group discussion, behavioural competency interviews, final interview are the steps in the process.
Division of Responsibility	High work burden of CC	Single-loop learning	With the transfer of the most of the institution building and group facilitation to the local community activists, CC is focusing mostly on building the activists, people's livelihoods and people's sub-projects.
Capacity Building of Staff	Training inputs not dovetailed with the emerging project needs.	Single-loop learning	Training to the CCs, APMs and DPMs now clearly linked to the pace of the project. Annual Schedules worked out.As the project progressed, the capacity building of VOs has begun, in addition to that of the SHGs and CIGs.
Project Implementation	Slow pace of CIF sub-projects	Single-loop learning	Initiation of Village livelihood action plans covering all poor and their multiple livelihoods in the project area has had a significant impact and accelerated the pace of CIF sub-projects.

Looking at the overall pattern of learning from process documentation, it appears that the majority of issues identified relate to project level, as single-loop learning. This may have been a limitation of the instrument itself, which focuses on the gap between what the institutional processes should be and what exists in practice. This preoccupation of the PMT may have restricted their thinking to the project boundaries project and prevented them from questioning basic assumptions. The process of learning was none the less useful in monitoring the project and bringing it on course.

Figure 4.1

Process of Learning within AP-DPIP

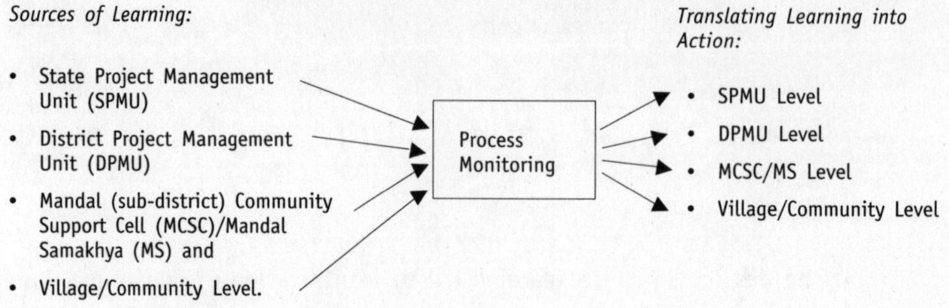

4.5.4 Key Messages

- Ensure quick access to information emerging from process monitoring.

The observations at each level emerging from PM are analysed then and there and shared with the concerned group/individuals who are responsible to act on it. For example, after having monitored the processes at the SHG level, the PMT shares the findings with the group and the activists/CCs who are responsible for the SHG's functioning. Participatory methods are adopted by the PMT, which facilitates immediate sharing of observations.

- Use existing project forums for learning.

The PM team was successful in converting the meetings at the district and state levels into learning forums. At each level, the PMT facilitates the group to agree on certain tasks. Cluster coordinators/asst. project managers are present with process monitoring team throughout the exercise. PMT also makes presentations on the observations to the SPMU during the PDs conference once in six months and also to the World Bank Supervision Mission during the visit to the state.

- Ensure compliance on PM findings

Right from the community level to the different layers of project management, an 'agreed to do' system has been established. Further, action taken reports have to be submitted to report on compliance.

- Integration with the MIS data

Since one of the objectives of PM was to assess the quality of the quantity, the MIS formed yet another important source of data collection.

4.6 Learning from a Community Group: CIG *Milans* in the District Poverty Initiatives Project (DPIP), Madhya Pradesh, India

District Poverty Initiative Project (DPIP)-MP is a World Bank assisted livelihood project being implemented in the state of Madhya Pradesh in Central India. The five-year project is being implemented in 2908 villages in 14 districts of the state. The main project activity involves creation of common interest groups (CIGs), formed from among the poorest families in project villages, which put forward a sub-project proposal for funding from DPIP. CIGs get up to 85 per cent of the cost of an activity as a grant, while the rest has to be generated by the group itself.

Action for Social Advancement (ASA), an Indian NGO experimented with the participatory monitoring and learning approach in the project when it was already half-way through completion. In contrast to the Andhra Pradesh case, ASA focused on creating learning forums starting at the community level. This case study is an example of how a community level group can play a monitoring role and contribute to learning within a project.

During the initial months of the PML experiment, discussions with the village communities and the project staff at various levels revealed several problems being encountered in the project:

- The number of CIGs had grown considerably over the years. At the same time, there was a pressure from the project to further increase the number of CIGs. This led to a situation where the project facilitating teams (PFT) (with a staff of 4-5) were finding it extremely difficult to maintain contact with the CIGs. It was also becoming difficult to pay attention to quality aspects, keep track of the performance of older CIGs, provide routine services such as assistance in book keeping, building market linkages, etc. In many cases, sub-project approval process was becoming more of an administrative requirement!
- At the village level, it was found that the *gram sabha* (village council, a constitutional local self-government body), which was expected to play a critical role in the governance and monitoring of CIGs, was, by and large ineffective. Originally, it was envisaged that a village development committee (VDC) would be formed within the project, which would be a representative body of the CIGs. However, the formation of VDC did not take place as originally planned and instead, it was felt that this role could be entrusted to existing *gram sabhas*.[2] However, the *gram sabhas* proved to be completely ineffective in performing this role. Further, in most cases, the CIGs, constituting of the poorest sections, did not have a voice in this forum. As a result, CIGs in most villages were unorganised and were devoid of the services of a mentor who could facilitate the process of CIG formation, activity

2. In January 2001, this move was in line with the passing of the Gramswaraj Adhiniyam Act of the Government of Madhya Pradesh, which empowered the *gram sabha* as supreme authority to plan, implement and monitor all developmental activities within the village. Thus DPIP's decision of enhancing the responsibility of the *gram sabha* was seen to complement the government's intent to strengthen and empower PRIs.

selection, provide a forum for interactions among CIGs, maintain link with the project and other stakeholders, etc. The local PFTs, were not able to provide these services, largely because of their preoccupation with achieving physical and financial targets.

4.6.1 The Genesis of CIG Milans and Learning Forums

The situation provided a clear-cut agenda for ASA, which felt that as a first step, there is a need to develop a forum (or a learning group) at the village level. Specifically, this forum would provide a platform to CIGs members to share their experiences for cross learning, encourage transparency at CIG level, identify problem issues, and feed this self-assessment and learning into project management and provide critical directions.

This gave rise to the concept of CIG *milans*, or a get-together of CIGs within a village, which was initiated in a large number of villages. A CIG *milan* can be defined as a periodic meeting (normally monthly or bimonthly) organised by a trained facilitator, who helped the CIGs to identify and articulate their problems, and explore solutions in a collaborative manner.

However, it was soon realised that creating *CIG milans* by itself was not enough. There was a need to set in place an institutional mechanism that would:

- encourage critical reflection at various levels within the project, starting with the community groups,
- allow feedback and lessons from experiences to be fed back into the decision making process within the project management system, and
- ensure that actions are taken on the basis of the above.

Hence, a system was set in place to establish learning forums at different levels that would critically reflect on issues emerging from discussions at CIG *milans* and act upon them. At the CIG *milans*, the CIGs were encouraged to resolve issues being faced by them. Lessons from CIG *milans* were systematically fed into the monthly review meeting of the DPSU (District Project Support Unit), an existing forum, where the PFTs (Project Facilitation Team) involved in the CIG *milans* were encouraged to make detailed presentations, based on reflections from the field. Hence, at the district level, a second round of screening of issues took place, and the issues that required policy changes were taken further up to the state project management. An institutional learning group was created at the state level, where inputs from CIG *milans* were shared.

4.6.2 Translating Learning into Action

The experience with CIG *milan* as a potential village-level governance forum has been extremely positive. In some villages, where the local NGO, contracted by the project to facilitate community mobilisation and following up on the CIG *milans*, the process was instrumental in initiating cross-learning and trouble shooting between groups.

ASA's initiative to create such a learning forum stems from its reflection on the learning process within the DPIP project system. It represents a case of triple-loop learning (TLL) which led to the formation of not only a learning forum for the local community but also a governance tool. Further, the forum generated feedback for the project implementation agency which was fed upwards by ASA's team at various levels for reflection and action.

It is interesting to note that during the initial meetings, the focus of discussion within CIG *milans* was entirely on resolving operational issues (SLL) faced by CIGs and the community was seeking quick solutions. Over time, as some of these were resolved and the community realised the potential of such a group, the emphasis shifted towards strategic issues (DLL), raised serious project level issues, which were taken up at district and state levels.

Decisions Taken on the Village Governance Issue Based on Learnings

By the SPSU:

- All PFTs to establish VDCs in two villages in their area, on a pilot basis.
- The project decided to recruit village resource persons, who would act as Secretary to VDC.

By the DPSU:

- The PFTs should identify potential candidates for village resource persons in villages where DPIP is in operation.
- In Chhatarpur (the district in which ASA was working), 14 villages are to be identified for forming VDCs on a pilot basis. Each PFT should identify two villages where more than 5 CIGs are functioning.

At the village/CIG level:

- To hold regular CIG *milans*.
- To assist each other in identifying problem areas and addressing areas of immediate concern.
- Making project information available to the community.
- Promoting transparency and accountability at CIG and project staff level.
- Decrease in the cost of sub-project value due to better awareness by the members from others who are already doing similar kind of sub-projects.

The experience clearly demonstrates the potential of this forum as a village-level governance body. At the village level, *CIG milans* were instrumental in:

- Resolving many of the operational issues and addressed areas of immediate concern.
- Making project information available to the community.
- Highlighting problems and achievements of CIGs.
- Promoting transparency and accountability at CIG and project staff level.

At the project level, the CIG *milan* can help in critical tasks such as:

- Helping the project staff develop a village perspective *vis-à-vis* DPIP.
- Assisting the project agencies in pre-screening of new CIG proposals.
- Providing warning signals regarding impending problems with specific CIGs so that timely corrective measures can be taken.
- Providing an opportunity for the project management to reflect on qualitative issues and initiate actions.
- Raising critical issues which need to be addressed through policy change.

The process of institutional learning as illustrated through the tackling of the governance issue at the village level is depicted schematically in the figure below:

Figure 4.2

Institutional Learning in MP-DPIP Project

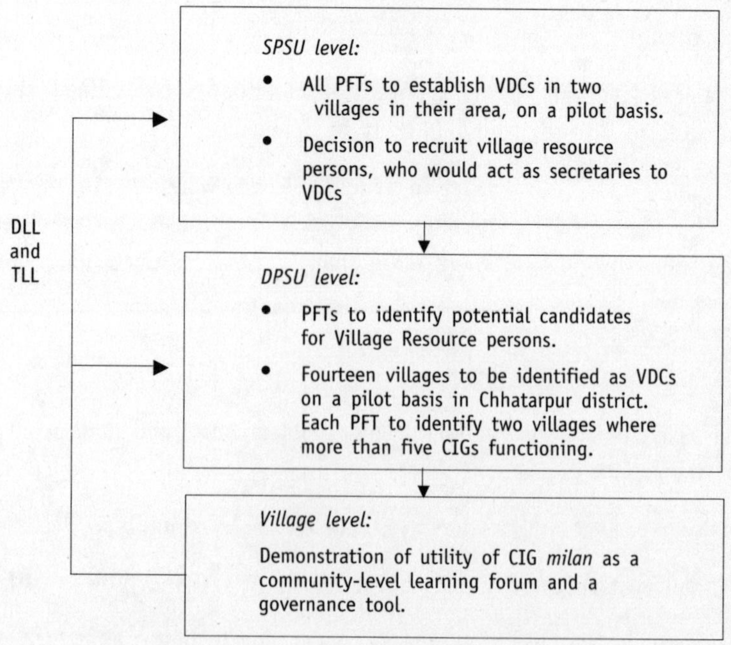

The figure shows how ASA's strategy to create a learning forum at the grassroots (through initial focus on the process of learning) represents a case of triple-loop learning. The realisation that the same forum could fill the void in governance at the villlage level represents double-loop learning. The figure shows how the internalisation of this critical learning led to action at the SPSU and DPSU levels. The creation of CIG *milans* on a larger scale, supported by village level resource persons led to learning of the SLL and DLL types which further strengthened the implementation and impacts of the project.

4.6.3 Key Messages

In MP-DPIP, ASA introduced PML only on a pilot scale but was able to identify the critical gaps in the learning system very quickly. This (triple-loop) learning was made possible by first making an assessment of the existing learning processes and systems within the implementing agency and its partners. Some lessons for using community-based participatory monitoring and learning effectively are:

- Build the facilitation skills of the field staff.

Specific areas for capacity building for the project staff who facilitate such meetings with the community groups include an understanding of local issues, conflict resolution, and complete information of the project.

- The process must result into tangible benefits for the project staff, especially at the field level.

In the DPIP experiment, the PFTs saw CIG *milans* as a forum that could assist them in their monitoring tasks which was becoming increasingly difficult. It also helped them in terms of reducing some of their workload.

- The community must be made to understand its role and shoulder its responsibility in the problem-solving process.

It must be made clear that the issues that can be resolved at the village level must be resolved there.

- Encourage critical reflection through learning forums.

Creation of learning forum at all levels is a must. To the extent possible, existing opportunities within the project structures must be utilised to encourage learning. In the ASA experiment, the existing mechanism of monthly DPSU meeting was used for sharing of findings.

Further reading on case studies:

ASA (2004). *Equitable and Sustainable Natural Resources Management through Participatory Monitoring,* A World Bank supported initiative in Madhya Pradesh, Inception Phase Report and Project Completion Report, Bhopal: Action for Social Advancement, 2003 and 2004.

CIP-SDC (1999). *Process Monitoring for Improving Sustainability, A Manual for Project Managers and Staff,* Published by the UNDP-World Bank Water and Sanitation Program-South Asia in collaboration with the Community Infrastructure Project and Swiss Agency for Development and Cooperation, July.

Guggenheim S, T. Wiranto, Y. Prasta and S. Wong (2004). "Indonesia Kecamatan Development Program: A Large-scale Use of Community Development to Reduce Poverty, A Case Study from Reducing Poverty, Sustaining Growth", *What Works, What Doesn't, and Why A Global Exchange for Scaling Up Success, Scaling Up Poverty Reduction*: A Global Learning Process and Conference, Shanghai, May 25-27.

UNDP–World Bank Water and Sanitation Program South Asia Region, *Improving Community Identification and Response in an Innovative Project: NWFP Community Infrastructure Project,* Field note.

Viloria, J. (SASIN) and M. Hosain (WSP-SA). *Transforming Organisations by Learning and Adaptation: Process Monitoring in the NWFP Community Infrastructure Project (CIP),* Participatory Monitoring & Evaluation, Good Practice & Lessons Learned. Downloaded from http://lnweb18.worldbank.org/sar/sa.nsf/attachments/tranforming/$file/tranforming.pdf.

Wong, Susan (2003). *Indonesia Kecamatan Development Program: Building a Monitoring and Evaluation System for a Large-scale Community-driven Development Program,* Environment and Social Development Unit, East Asia and Pacific Region, World Bank, May.

World Bank (2003). Implementation Completion Report (IDA-28290 COFN-03700 PPFI-P7610) Report No: 27496, for the NWFP Community Infrastructure and NHA Strengthening Project, December 31, Rural Development, South Asia Region.

Websites:

www.velugu.org

www.jalanidhi.com

http://www.dpipmp.nic.in

http://kar.nic.in//watershed/sujala

Annexures

ANNEXURE A-1

THE WORLD BANK PROJECT CYCLE

The World Bank project cycle essentially involves four stages of Identification, Preparation, Appraisal, Implementation and Supervision and the Evaluation phases. Each of these phases is further broken down into discrete steps, which are described below:

The Identification Phase

After a project has been incorporated into the lending programme, it enters the project pipeline, and an extensive period normally one to two years—of close collaboration between the Bank and the eventual borrower begins. Once a project has been identified, the Bank team creates a Project Concept Note (PCN). The PCN is an internal document of four to five pages that outlines the basic elements of the project, its proposed objective, likely risks, alternative scenarios to conducting the project, and a likely timetable for the project approval process.

The Project Information Document (PID) is prepared after an internal review of the PCN and is released publicly. It is usually four to five pages long and contains information on the objective, a brief description, etc.

The Integrated Safeguards Data Sheet (ISDS) is prepared after the project's first formal review and made available publicly. It identifies key issues under the World Bank's safeguard policies for environmental and social issues, and provides information about how they will be addressed during project preparation.

The Preparation Phase

The formal responsibility for preparation lies with the borrower, and this part of the process can take anything from a few months to three years, depending on the complexity of the project being proposed. The Bank plays a supporting role, offering analysis and advice where requested, making sure that the borrower understands the Bank's requirements and standards and filling in gaps in projects. During this period, the technical, institutional, economic, environmental and financial issues facing the project are studied and addressed—including whether there are alternative methods for achieving the same objectives. An assessment is required of projects proposed for Bank financing to help ensure that they are environmentally sound and sustainable (Environmental Assessment). The scope of the Environmental Assessment depends on the scope, scale and potential impact of the project.

The preparation phase documents that are produced include an Environmental Assessment Report (EA) which analyses the likely environmental impact of a planned project and steps to mitigate possible harm, an Indigenous Peoples Development Plan which identifies potentially adverse effects on the health, productive resources, economies, and cultures of indigenous peoples, and the Environmental Action Plan which describes the major environmental concerns of a country, identifies the main causes of problems, and formulates policies and concrete actions to deal with the problems.

The Appraisal Phase

The Bank is responsible for this part of the process. Bank staff reviews the work done during identification and preparation. They prepare for bank management Project Appraisal Documents and the Financial Management Team assesses the financial aspects of the project. The PID is updated during this phase. These documents are released to the public after the project is approved.

After Bank staff members have appraised the proposed project, the Bank and the country that is seeking to borrow the funds, negotiate on its final shape. Both sides come to an agreement on the terms and conditions of the loan. Then the Project Appraisal Document (PAD), along with the Memorandum of the President and legal documents are submitted to the Bank's Board of Executive Directors for approval. The appropriate documents are also submitted for final clearance by the borrowing government which may involve ratification by a council of ministers or a country's legislature. Following approval by both parties, the loan agreement is formally signed by their representatives. Once this has occurred, the loan or credit is declared effective, or ready for disbursement, after the relevant conditions are met, and the agreement is made available to the public.

The PAD presents all the information the Board needs to approve Bank financing of the proposal. Before 1999, this document was called the Staff Appraisal Report.

At this stage, the borrower is expected to prepare the Project Implementation Plan or the PIP, which details out the roles and responsibilities of the various players in the project implementation, the timelines, and budgetary allocations. This is the working document for the borrower and the project implementing agency, which is used throughout the project period, as a reference document and guide.

The Implementation and Supervision Phase

The implementation of the project is the responsibility of the borrowing country, while the Bank is responsible for supervision. Once the loan is approved, the borrowing government, with technical assistance from the Bank, prepares the specifications and evaluates bids for the procurement of goods and services for the project. The Bank reviews this activity to ensure that its procurement guidelines have been followed. If they have, the funds will be disbursed. The Bank's Financial Management Team maintains an oversight of the financial management of the project including periodically requiring audited financial statements.

Report on the Status of Projects in Execution provides a very brief summary of all projects that were active during the previous fiscal year. Previously an internal communication to the Board of Executive Directors, the SOPE report now is available to the public. Projects that closed during the fiscal year are no longer included in the SOPE, since their implementation completion reports are also publicly disclosed.

For every completed project, an implementation completion report identifying accomplishments, problems, and lessons learned is prepared by the Bank staff.

The Evaluation Phase

Following the completion of a project, the Bank's Operations Evaluation Department conducts an audit to measure its outcome against the original objectives.

The audit entails a review of the project completion report and preparation of a separate report. Both reports are then submitted to the executive directors and the borrower. They are not released to the public.

Project Performance Assessment Reports rate project outcomes (taking into account relevance, efficacy, and efficiency), sustainability of results, and the institutional development impact. One in four completed projects (or about 70 a year) is chosen for a Project Performance Assessment Report, which takes Operations and Evaluation Department staff about six weeks to produce and normally includes a visit to the project in the borrowing country.

Impact Evaluation Reports assess the economic worth of projects and the long-term effects on people and the environment. These 'second looks' at projects are performed five to eight years after the close of loan disbursements.

Inspection Panel Reports review claims by affected parties that the Bank failed to follow its operational policies and procedures with respect to the design, appraisal and/or implementation of a Bank-financed operation.

ANNEXURE A-2

TAMIL NADU EMPOWERMENT AND POVERTY REDUCTION PROJECT: MONITORING AND LEARNING SYSTEM

The Tamil Nadu Empowerment and Poverty Reduction Project (TNEPRP) supports Government of Tamil Nadu's (GoTN) strategy for reducing poverty among the rural poor and other vulnerable groups. The project consists of the following components: 1) Building institutional capacity, synergising and strengthening pro-poor local institutions and fund productive livelihood related investments at the village level. 2) Strengthening the project teams and supporting organisations at the state and district levels to respond to the needs of the poor and build institutional linkages and livelihood options for enhanced sustainability of the livelihoods of the poor and vulnerable. 3) Facilitating overall coordination, implementation, monitoring and learning of the project at state and district levels.

The M&L system shall have five distinct components, namely (i) Baseline, (ii) Performance tracking, (iii) Institutional performance tracking, (iv) Internal learning, and (v) Impact evaluation. In the following paragraphs each of these components are discussed in detail.

Table A-2.1

Summary of M&L System

M&L Components	*Information Collected On*	*Instrument*	*Type of Data*	*Frequency*	*By Whom*
Performance Tracking	1. Project inputs/ activities 2. Key performance indicators (as per project results framework)	1. Pro-forma, computerised MIS 2. Six monthly external studies	1. Quantitative 2. Qualitative	1. Monthly/ quarterly 2. Six monthly	1. PFT-DPU (District Project Unit)-SPU (State Project Unit) 2. External
Institutional Performance Tracking	Institutional performances of CBOs	Assessment against institutional development indicators	Qualitative	Annual	DM&LC (District Monitoring and Learning Coordinator) with PFT
Internal Learning	Project processes	1. CPML* 2. PML**	Qualitative	1. Quarterly 2. Quarterly	1. External 2. Internal
Evaluation	Project outcomes and impacts	Impact study	Qualitative	Mid-term and post project	External
Baseline	Pre-project conditions	Baseline	Quantitative and qualitative	Before project	External

Note: * Concurrent Process Monitoring and Learning.
** Participatory Monitoring and Learning.

(i) Baseline: The objective of the baseline is to establish the net contribution of the project to the sustainable livelihoods of the targeted families 'before' and 'after' the project and 'between' the project and control areas. The baseline will consist of (a) A hypothesis document for identifying key hypotheses regarding demand for different types of project interventions by specific groups and the impact of such interventions and the methodology to measure them; (b) Sampling document for describing the methodology adopted for baseline survey including control and surveyed areas, justification for choosing samples and size of sample, basis for weights, etc.; and (c) Questionnaires for households, beneficiary local governments, and village leaders with retrospective questions wherever appropriate.

An independent agency would be contracted to undertake the baseline survey. The agency selected needs to have required capacity and experience to design, implement and analyse large scale surveys.

(ii) Performance Tracking: Would cover inputs, outputs and outcomes of the project. Input/output monitoring is required to assess the service standards and for the resource accountability. The outcome tracking is mainly for validating project's hypotheses for achieving project development goal. The performance monitoring would consist of progress monitoring which will track project progress against the planned activities on a monthly basis. This will be mainly the numbers of either initiation or completion of activities. The second part of the performance monitoring will be for measuring the progress of project on the qualitative aspects, especially, against the key performance indicators.

The progress or activity monitoring will be done through review meetings and pro-forma reporting. The data on the initiation and completion of activity would be collected for each component/sub-component, *viz.*

- Geographic, demographic, coverage of socio-economic, vulnerable groups, SC/STs, etc;
- Project funds, human resources, capacity building, services provided, etc;
- Number of SHGs/CIGs/VPRCs/PLF formed, etc.

The primary data would be collected on monthly, quarterly and six monthly bases depending upon the nature of inputs and its maturity through pro-forma by the PFT. A Computerised Management Information System (CMIS) will be established which will do the necessary processing of primary data once entered and make it available to all levels of project management in the analysed form and also in aggregated and disaggregated form by operational unit of management. The CMIS will be web based and can be accessed at all levels of project management including the World Bank. This data would be used for periodic review of project progress at the cluster, district and state level and will serve the purpose of reporting by the project to the GoTN, GoI and the World Bank.

The performance monitoring against the key performance indicators will be done by an external agency on every sixth month, called Six-monthly Performance Monitoring. The project would also commission theme based studies for detail understanding of the issues that might have been flagged or alerted by the M&L system.

Setting up, operationalisation of CMIS and the commissioning of Six-monthly Performance Monitoring study will be the responsibility of the M&L cell of the State Project Unit (SPU).

(iii) Institutional Performance Tracking: The central objective of this component would be to assess the performances of the different project induced CBOs (e.g. SHG, CIGs, PLF, Federations, VPRCs) against a set of Institutional Development Indicators (IDI). The Institutional Performance Tracking would monitor CBOs on the parameters such as characteristics, identity and structure leadership, functioning, etc.

The M&L cell in due course will develop set of IDIs for each type of the community institutions it promotes.

The institutional performance tracking would be undertaken annually for all types of community institutions. The results of institutional performance tracking would be shared at all levels of project organisations. This would trigger off special studies and designing/redesigning of project inputs for institutional capacity building.

This will be an internal functioning of the project's M&L unit. Under the direction of State M&L Specialist (SM&LS) the District M&L Specialist will be responsible to accomplish this component on a timely basis with the help of the PFTs and other front-line staff of the project. The PFTs and the front-line staff would be trained to facilitate the process at the CBO level in a fashion that it becomes a learning experience for the CBOs for them to undertake corrective measures.

(iv) Internal Learning: Internal learning is crucial for the project to be responsive to the changing context of the project as it moves forward. The internal learning component of the M&L system would consist of:

(a) Concurrent Process Monitoring and Learning (CPML), and

(b) Participatory Monitoring and Learning (PML)

The formation and institutionalisation of Learning Groups (LGs) at different levels would be the key for internal learning to be effective. A three-tier system of LGs are envisaged involving stakeholders of the project at different levels. These LGs will be dovetailed within the existing institutional structures created for project management. The LGs will be created at the village/GP level called Community Learning Group (CLG), and at the district and state level called District Learning Group (DLG) and Institutional Learning Group (ILG) respectively. A systematic facilitation will be made to these LGs periodically for them to assimilate learning and to refine conclusions and encourage suggestions/decisions for changes where required. The members in these learning groups shall be as following:

Table A-2.1

Learning Groups	*Community Learning Groups (CLG)*	*District Learning Groups (DLG)*	*Institutional Learning Groups (ILG)*
Level	Village	District	State
Members	The *gram sabha* including members of GP, VPRC, SHG, ABG, ABF, PLF and community at large	DPU, PFTs, capacity bldg. organisation,	PD & SPU staff, consultants
Anchor	Social Audit Committee with the help from PFT	District M&L Specialist (DMLS)	State M&L Specialist (SMLS)

Note: If required the learning group at the cluster level can also be developed involving all VPRCs, PLF, CLFs and PFTs of that cluster.

(a) Concurrent Process Monitoring and Learning (CPML)

TNEPRP is a process intensive project. The culmination of outcomes of the project would depend mainly on the strength of the processes adopted. Therefore, CPML would be undertaken to help the project management and others involved to understand how and through what process inputs get converted into outputs, what issues are critical in that conversion process and what action is necessary to increase effectiveness. CPML would, therefore, verify the quality of the project implementation on a continuous basis.

The monitorable issues on which project needs qualitative assessment can be broadly divided in to two categories—(i) project management and organisational development related issues; and (ii) field implementation related issues. Some examples of the issues under these two categories are:

(i) Project management and organisational development related issues

- Staff recruitment and their capacity building
- Staffing at different project management unit
- Relationship between different levels of project management
- Role clarity of staff, sensitivity of staff towards the need of vulnerable group *viz.* poor, women, disabled, etc.
- Sub-project proposal appraisal process

(ii) Field implementation related issues

- Sub project proposal preparation, process of preparation of livelihood plan
- Inclusiveness in planning, execution and benefits sharing
- Formation and institutional performance of GPs and other project induced CBOs *viz.* VPRCs, SHGs, CIGs, etc.

An external agency will be contracted to conduct CPML. The reasons for engaging external agency are (a) bringing in objectivity to the exercise, and (b) to deal with the constraints of lack of capacity of internal staff and avoiding biases in the findings that might come into play.

The process of CPML would start with the identification of monitorable processes, process steps and their corresponding indicators. The processes will be identified on the basis of their criticality to the project. This will be done in consultation with the project staff annually in a workshop facilitated by the CPML agency. As a next step the levels of CPML to be determined for each of the identified processes (i.e. at what level the CPML is to be conducted. For instance, CPML for issues-like staff recruitment and capacity building will be carried out at the state and district level, where as CPML for sub-project proposal appraisal or fund disbursement to VPRC shall include the village and district levels only).

The agency contracted for CPML will have staff positioned at the district level and they will collect data on the identified processes on a regular basis. For the field implementation related processes, where community is involved, data will be collected using participatory appraisal tools like FGDs, self-assessment, stakeholders' meetings, etc. The benefit of using participatory tools is that the data providers will get on the spot analysis of the information provided by them. The data collected will then be analysed along with the observations by the CPML team. The findings and observations of CPML will be shared at the LGs (CLG, DLG, ILG) as appropriate (as per the levels determined) for the issue/s concerned for them to assimilate learning and take corrective actions. This process will be followed on a quarterly basis. The CPML will prepare report for each round including process discussion, concerns/gaps and suggested action and prepare Action Required Report for the project management to follow up.

The CPML will be an ongoing process along side the project implementation. About 10 per cent of the project villages will be covered under CPML. The Monitoring and Learning study which is undergoing currently will develop detail strategy including the sampling.

b) Participatory Monitoring and Learning (PML)

PML is a process through which stakeholders especially the primary stakeholders are engaged in monitoring project's processes and results. In practical terms, PML is a set of participatory tools and methods for measuring, assessing, reporting on, and ultimately improving organisation's social performance through institutional learning. It can bring stakeholders together in assessing project progress and to focus better on project outputs and impacts from the viewpoint of equity and sustainability, thereby enhancing the accountability and efficiency of project institutions.

The PML process would broadly involve the following steps:

- Selection of PML themes/issues in consultation with the community and the project staff. The issues may vary from district to district. Any attempt to standardisation of issues and indicators and expecting community to reflect upon them will be a kind imposition on them and therefore the real issues bothering the community and implementation may not be surfaced. To deal with such disperse situation it is therefore planned that the district will identify one or few PML themes/issues for a particular period, preferably for a quarter. The point to be noted is that social audit, group's self-assessment will be some of the PML issues taken up in regular interval.

- Based on the theme the PML team will look into various issues that are existing in a village and which can be explored for PML. From the experiences it is found that both the local communities as well as project functionaries at the grassroots level proved to be valuable sources for identifying issues. The field functionaries are generally aware of the issues faced by different stakeholder groups. Community level meetings also help to generate issues as well as data related to a particular issue at the same time.

- Finalisation of issues to be taken up for the PML for the quarter. As a strategy, such issues will be given priority in the initial stage of PML which are non-threatening in nature in order to generate confidence in the PML process.

- Issue exploration by collecting data through applying standard participatory tools. This would require consultation with the different stakeholder groups in the village (especially the vulnerable groups who can not express their views due to skewed power equations in the village) and getting their perspective on the issue. The regular M&E data will also be used whenever required to substantiate findings. Care will be taken that data collection process itself becomes an enabling process for the data providers to analyse situations and learn.

- Presentation of findings to the CLG in a village-level workshop. The PFT should be anchoring the process with active support from the PML team. Facilitation of CLG meeting will be done in a manner that issues are presented with right perspective and good discussion takes place on them. Experience suggests that many of the operational issues, felt and unfelt, will be resolved in the CLG meeting itself. Certain issues surfaced during the process would require strategic and policy support from the district and state level. The CLG meeting would conclude with the preparation of an Action Required Report (ARR) with clearly spelt out responsibilities of the project staff and community members.

- The findings of CLG meetings will be shared with the DLG in a workshop organised quarterly by the PML team. Issues will be classified into those that can be addressed (or have been addressed) at the CLG or village level (which the PFT will be responsible for), those that need intervention at the District Project Unit level (for which the DM&LS will be responsible for follow up), and policy issues that need to be discussed at the state level, which will be communicated to the SM&LS.

- The SM&LS will conduct an ILG meeting at the state level once a quarter, in which he/she will make a presentation to the ILG, identifying issues emerging from CLG and DLG that need to be addressed at the state level.

- The follow up of the decisions/action points made at the DLG meeting and the ILG will be done through ATRs (Action Taken Report) submitted by the DM&LS and the SM&LS to the DPM and the PD respectively, once every quarter.

Findings/learning coming out of all other initiatives like CPML, CBO performance monitoring, community score card, process learning through experience sharing or any other such initiatives being taken by the project to promote internal learning should be shared at these LGs quarterly depending upon the relevance of the subject to that level.

The overall coordination of PML activity at the district and state level will be the responsibility of DM&LS and SM&LS respectively.

(v) Impact Evaluation: Impact evaluation would involve comparing qualitative and quantitative outcomes before and after the project and between project and control areas. The impact and outcome indicators will be the point of reference to establish the net effect of the project. The impact evaluation would consider major assumptions to establish causal relationship between input, outputs and outcomes. The impact evaluation study would require rigorous methodology and quality analysis. An independent agency, perhaps the same agency involved in baseline study, will be contracted for the impact study in control and project villages on sample basis.

ANNEXURE A-3

Indicative Contents list for Documentation of the M&E Section in the Project Implementation Plan (PIP)

1. **Purpose and scope of the M&E system**
   - Project background
   - Rationale for the design of the learning-based M&E system
   - Identification of key stakeholders
   - Key performance questions, indicators and information needs
   - How the M&E system, including the learning component, will support the project management system and meet the needs of the different stakeholders
   - Extent and feasibility of community participation in monitoring and learning
2. **Approach**
   - Roles of different stakeholders in the proposed learning-based M&E system
   - What approaches including information gathering and analysis methods will be used?
   - Integration with the overall M&E and reporting system
3. **Work-plan for the learning-based M&E system**
   - Key processes, events and timing of activities
   - Definition of methods to be used with different stakeholder groups
   - Components of the system: institutional assessment, evaluations, process monitoring
4. **MIS and reporting**
   - Organisation of information gathering and synthesis (for each information—who, what, when, where, data storage system)
   - Use of participatory/non-participatory methods
   - Level of aggregation/segregation and the feedback mechanism
   - Reporting and communication including feedback channels, reports to be produced (deadlines and frequencies)
5. **Establishing conditions and capacities**
   - M&L organisation within the project implementing agency
   - Need and role of external facilitating agency (including sample ToR for M&L facilitating agency)

- Human resource needs (number, capacities and responsibilities of different stakeholders including project staff and primary stakeholders, incentives, training needs)
- Resource needs (technical assistance, equipment)

Indicative Contents list for Documentation of the M&E Section in the PAD

- M&E purpose and scope in the project context including the information needs of the project stakeholders
- Key performance questions, indicators and information collection requirements
- Components of the learning-based M&E system: internal institutional assessment (key processes and tasks and events), evaluations, process monitoring, and its integration with the M&E information
- Structure and staffing for M&E (approximation of staffing levels and types, organisational structure of M&E and its interaction mechanism with the project management)
- Capacity building (approximation of support required for smooth operation of M&E)
- Budgetary requirements

ANNEXURE A-4

TERMS OF REFERENCE FOR NGO INDEPENDENT MONITORING OF KDP

A. Background

The Kecamatan Development Programme (KDP) is a Government of Indonesia programme aimed at alleviating poverty in rural communities and improving local governance. KDP provides block grants of 350 million to one billion rupiah ($40,000 to $114,000) directly to kecamatan and villages for small-scale infrastructure, social and economic activities. KDP's monitoring and evaluation system consists of several components:

- Monthly field reporting from consultants at the *kecamatan, kabupaten*, provincial and national levels
- Complaints/problems monitoring and resolution
- Community participatory monitoring
- Monitoring by government officials
- Case studies documenting best practices and lessons learned
- Special studies on infrastructure, economic activities, and other themes
- Financial supervision and auditing
- Joint World Bank/GoI supervision missions
- Impact studies
- Independent monitoring and reporting by the Association of Independent Journalists (AJI)

In order to strengthen its monitoring system, KDP will invite Indonesian NGOs to monitor independently programme progress in each province. This activity is intended to provide valuable inputs for improving the programme.

B. Description of NGO Independent Monitoring

The purpose of the NGO independent monitoring is to provide an independent source of qualitative information on KDP implementation from a select number of project locations to complement the information collected through the project's internal monitoring system.

Currently, KDP monitoring centres on regular internal reporting from project implementors at all project locations. Although the reporting system is effective for monitoring progress on programme implementation, inputs, and direct outputs, it is less effective at registering the programme's ability to affect less tangible changes (such as improvements in the quality of women's participation and institutional strengthening), and a wide range of specific problems and lessons learned from overcoming them. Also, because all information stems from programme staff, data is not collected by objective parties. In order to ensure that emerging problems are noted and addressed, additional monitoring is required to provide data on: (i) common problems that are occurring in many or all locations; (ii) specific problems limited to a particular location; and (iii) short and medium-term changes brought about by the programme. The NGO independent monitoring described herein mainly concerns the collection of qualitative data through participatory methods, although a small number of quantitative indicators will also be incorporated in the NGO monitoring. The main source of information will be villagers and stakeholders in KDP *kecamatan*, both those that have participated directly in the programme and others who have not. Some data may be collected at the *kecamatan* level, but only as they relate to programme implementation at the village level.

C. Specific Tasks and Responsibilities

NGO independent monitoring is currently planned for all 22 KDP provinces. NGOs will monitor regularly the programme's developments and provide an independent source of information to improve KDP. The primary users of the collected information will be province and district-based project staff. The NGO monitoring is not intended to cover all project areas; the emphasis is on the NGO to provide rich, descriptive information in a sample of select locations. In each chosen province, one or two NGOs (or NGO consortia) will be identified to carry out the monitoring. The Community Development Office in the Ministry of Home Affairs (PMD), the National Management Consultants (NMC) and World Bank will select the NGOs on a competitive basis.

1. Monitoring Scope

NGOs will focus on these specific areas for monitoring:

- participation of villagers, especially women and the poor, in all phases of the programme;
- information-sharing and transparency;
- adherence with the general principles and procedures of the programme;
- quality of technical assistance;
- quality of programme outputs;
- financial review; and
- recommendations from programme stakeholders to improve KDP.

2. Geographic Coverage

In most provinces, only one NGO or NGO consortia will be chosen for each province. Each month, the NGO must visit a total of eight villages in a minimum of three *kecamatan*. Two villages should be monitored continuously each month (through community participatory monitoring) in order to follow the progress of the complete project cycle in two set locations. The NGO can select any other six villages to visit. The NGO should rotate its monitoring of *kecamatan* and districts so that it covers as wide an area as possible (taking into account budgetary considerations). The NGO should try to monitor a wide sample of KDP locations in various sites around the province.

Summary of Monitoring Each Month:

- District : Sample as many districts as possible.
- Kecamatan: Minimum of three *kecamatan.*
- Village: Minimum of eight villages, monitor two villages continuously, monitor six other villages.

3. Methodology To Be Used

The NGO shall decide what monitoring tools it wishes to use. Some monitoring and data collection tools include:

- Direct Observation
- Informal interviews
- Focus Group Discussions
- Mini-surveys
- Participatory rural appraisal
- Community participatory monitoring
- Financial review of book-keeping

Community participatory monitoring will be required in the two villages that are continuously monitored each month. Using this methodology, the NGO will facilitate the community members in data collection, compiling questions and analysing their data. The NMC will provide training on these methodologies at the start of the contract. Monitoring should include direct observation of the various stages of the planning process (such as observing village and *kecamatan*-level meetings), as well as more general monitoring of developments at the village level (such as informal discussions with villagers about their involvement in the KDP process). NGOs should make a special point of interviewing the poorer segments of the community to solicit their views on KDP and the process. Direct quotations from the field are highly encouraged and should be included in the NGO reports.

Under this ToR, NGOs will also be responsible for financial monitoring and checking simple book-keeping at the *kecamatan* and village levels. While a full-scale audit is not required, the NGO will be expected to spot-check financial documentation and be on the lookout for cases of corruption or price mark-ups.

The NGO should strive to be as thorough as possible in its monitoring. It should cross-check its findings and determine the validity of the information with a range of sources, including villagers, contractors, government officials, and consultants. It is important to note that the implementing organisation's role is to observe, collect, analyse, and report data. The NGO must not compromise its independent observer status by intervening to correct perceived problems or otherwise become involved in the process. The role of the NGO is to monitor the process and then report its findings to KDP implementers.

4. Analysis of Collected Information

NGOs will clean and analyse the collected data, drawing attention to problems encountered, villagers' recommendations for changes, and general findings of programme impacts. NGOs are expected not only to present field findings but also to analyse systematically the results and provide recommendations.

5. Reporting

During the first week of each month, the NGO will make an oral presentation of findings to provincial KDP consultants and the government coordination teams. In addition, the NGO will submit a brief written report on the previous month's monitoring results to them. The main text of the report should be no more than 10 pages in length, followed by attachments.

E. Management and Contract Provisions

Upon selection, NGOs will be asked to attend a national orientation about KDP, led by NMC staff, to be introduced to project objectives, design, and procedures. A range of monitoring methodologies will also be reviewed. NGOs will then be asked to finalise a time schedule and work-plan for the monitoring activities. The NGOs' main counterparts for the provincial monitoring will be the KDP field consultants, although KDP central-based staff will be directly involved at early stages to provide feedback on reports as well as provide technical assistance and guidance throughout the monitoring process. The contract will be signed between PMD[1] and the contracting NGO for an initial one-year period. That contract is subject to renewal after one year depending upon contract performance and availability of funds. The NGO will negotiate a lump-sum fee contract with PMD. Payments to NGOs will be made in three installments. Thirty per cent of the total fee will be paid out at the initiation of the contract. An additional 60 per cent of the total fee will be paid based upon receipt and acceptance of the first three monthly reports. The remaining 10 per cent of the total fee will be paid after all 12 reports have been submitted as agreed.

---

1. Pembangunan Masyarakat Desa, or the Community Development Agency under the Ministry of Home Affairs. PMD is the government implementing agency for KDP.

ANNEXURE A-5

KECAMATAN DEVELOPMENT PROJECT, INDONESIA: MONTHLY REPORTING SYSTEM BY FIELD CONSULTANTS

The monthly reporting formats varied depending upon the field position, but generally covered the following topics:

- activities completed during the past month and plans for the following month;
- status of activities in the project cycle;
- description of infrastructure, economic and social activities;
- financial information;
- level of community participation in activities;
- information dissemination and transparency;
- training and activities with village councils, *kecamatan* financial units and other local institutions;
- coordination work with government coordination teams, parliaments, and other government agencies;
- coordination with NGOs, journalists, or other civil society groups;
- problems encountered and proposed solutions;
- any other issues; and
- attachments: reporting forms, photos, complaints received, etc.

Field staff sent their monthly reports directly to their companies for forwarding to the Ministry of Home Affairs, with copies to their local field supervisors and the NMC[1] in Jakarta, which was responsible for technical supervision of field consultants. The regional coordinators at the NMC reviewed the reports and quantitative data was entered into an ACCESS Management Information System in Jakarta. The NMC and PMD used the monthly reports to assess progress in the project cycle, monitor financial disbursements, and keep track of problems arising in the field. The NMC also encouraged field staff to review their progress reports at the monthly provincial and district level coordination meetings.

---

1. National Management Consultants, located at central level.